ΛΛ AMERICAN **MARKETING** ASSOCIATION

THE

OBSERVATIONAL

RESEARCH

HANDBOOK

BILL ABRAMS

UNDERSTANDING HOW CONSUMERS
LIVE WITH YOUR PRODUCT

NTC

NTC Business Books
NTC/Contemporary Publishing Group

Library of Congress Cataloging-in-Publication Data

Abrams, Bill.
    The observational research handbook : understanding how consumers live with your product / Bill Abrams.
        p.   cm.
    At head of title: American Marketing Association.
    Includes bibliographical references.
    ISBN 0-658-00073-X
        1. Consumer behavior—United States.   2. Marketing—United States.
    I. Title.   II. American Marketing Association.
    HF5415.33.U6 A25   2000
    658.8'34 21—dc21   99-044308
                                                                    CIP

Interior design by Monica Baziuk
Interior page layout/typesetting by Pamela Juárez

Published by NTC Business Books
(in conjunction with the American Marketing Association)
A division of NTC/Contemporary Publishing Group, Inc.
4255 West Touhy Avenue, Lincolnwood (Chicago), Illinois 60712-1975 U.S.A.
Printed in the United States of America
International Standard Book Number: 0-658-00073-X
    01 02 03 04 LB 19 18 17 16 15 14 13 12 11 10 9 8 7 6 5 4 3 2

To Ariel Allen—the first to try an untried methodology

CONTENTS

FOREWORD

Early in 1999 an article appeared in the London *Evening Standard*. It read, in part as follows:

> *The hottest qualifications for corporate highlifers is no longer the law degree from Harvard or the business studies certificate from Massachusetts Institute of Technology. . . . American companies eager to squeeze evermore dollars out of a booming economy are racing to sign up anthropology graduates in the belief that they bring an insight into money making that business schools alone fail to do.*

As Katherine Ryan, head of money managers for the Hanseatic Group, put it, "Preconceptions can kill you. Anthropology is all about observation. That's what we do—observe."

That's what Bill Abrams does—since about 1983.

I was fortunate enough to hire Abrams for an all-too-brief teaching stint at the University of Illinois. One of the many things that made him attractive to us was his pioneering research agenda—taking qualitative research well beyond the popular focus group and lifestyle surveys. Now that we may all benefit from his wealth of experience and insight in book form, I feel increasingly compelled to place Abrams in historical context, particularly in relation to a researcher named Ernest Dichter. Dichter, a Freudian-trained psychologist, hit his stride during the booming postwar economy, when the consumer was inundated by a plethora of new products, many of them having parity. Marketers of the time were increasingly troubled about how to secure a competitive edge. Dichter and contemporaries such as the *Chicago Tribune*'s Pierre Martineau got attention by asking the right question: "Why do consumers become brand loyal in an undifferentiated market?"

There are, I believe, parallels with Bill's work. First, a remarkable late-century economy has left us awash with products and services, and has afforded the consumer virtually endless choices—among and within product classes. Just as in Dichter's time, today's marketers are seeking an edge through packaging, advertising, promotion, price, and product design. Then as now more fail than succeed. The observational research of today, like the "motivational research" of Dichter's day, asks questions that could provide the nuanced edge for profitable differentiations. And, again like motivational research, observational research seeks those answers through a deep understanding of how people interact with products and services.

However, Dichter's and Abrams's approaches to developing this deep understanding differ. Dichter's techniques, seeking psychological insights through the wellspring of consumer motivation, were those of psychoanalysis: depth interviews, thematic apperception tests, and "psychodramas." Observational research, by contrast, seeks clues from the study of consumer *behavior* under natural conditions. The resulting insights can be rich indeed:

- How real people navigate—or crash—when trying to bring their computer mouse in productive proximity to just the right icon

- How a simple dimple in a shampoo bottle turned out to be a key (and totally unplanned) factor in consumer choice

- How observing a family at mealtime led to a clear revelation about who should be targeted for a food product—a highly productive insight confirmed (but buried) in earlier quantitative studies

As market niches become the reality of our marketplace—with the promise of individualized selling in the twenty-first century—qualitative research offering understanding of how people actually *use* consumer goods *in their real worlds* will clearly become far more important than even its current ascendancy would suggest. And, among those rich qualitative tools, observational research may very well become the tool of choice.

The pages ahead will tell you about what has been—and can be—done with the ideas and techniques of observational research. You are fortunate to have as your guide not only a pioneer in the field, but also—trust me on this one!—a remarkable teacher.

Partake!

Dr. Kim Rotzoll
Dean, College of Communications
The University of Illinois at
Urbana-Champaign

ACKNOWLEDGMENTS

I want to thank my patient, perceptive editor, Danielle Egan-Miller; Mal Bybee, whose reading of the original manuscript opened my perspective; and the following people for their invaluable help and advice: Roslyn Arnstein, Lorrie Browning, Jorge Calvachi, Carol Christensen, Elizabeth Ellers, Jim Figura, Arthur Fox, Kathy Hennesy, Kim Rotzoll, and Nina Sweet. And I have to thank the marvelous professionals who have worked with me on so many Housecalls assignments: Janet Allen, Pat Kirmayer, Terri Marlowe, Roland Millman, and Stella Varveris.

INTRODUCTION

In 1983, I was creative director on the Colgate-Palmolive account at Kenyon & Eckhardt Advertising (now part of Bozell World Wide.) For almost all of my professional life I had strongly relied on research to tell me and the people who worked with me what consumers were like, how they used the products and services we were advertising, why they stayed loyal to one product and not another, what benefits and what negatives they saw in them, and what we could say that would make them or keep them interested in the brands we worked on.

I literally can't count how many focus groups I've attended or mall interviews I've conducted to learn everything I could about the relationship between consumers and the products they use. Unlike many creative directors who believed solely in their own intuitions, way before I started the creative process I used qualitative research to soak up as much information as possible about the ways people live with products. I believed my intuition worked best when it had reliable information to feed on.

But in the early eighties I started to notice something strange. I don't know why I hadn't picked up on it before. My writers and art directors who were attending those focus groups with me were among the best, most professional creative people in the country.

But were they watching, were they listening to the consumers sitting around the table on the other side of the two-way mirror? Not much. Most of the time they spent telling jokes to each other, munching on the sandwiches provided by the facility, or making phone calls back to New York. One guy even brought a novel to read at a focus group. My colleagues were downright bored. What was going on here? Why were these gifted, motivated advertising people not watching and not listening? Why were they turning a deaf ear and a blind eye to the reams of consumer information pouring through the mirror and the microphone?

The reason finally struck me. My writers and art directors were experiencing these focus groups as a kind of nonreality, as something artificial. What they were witnessing—when they deigned to look and listen—was the consumer *memory* of the product experience and not the experience itself. And it was a selective memory at that, often bent way out of shape even as the respondents recalled it, to make themselves look good to other members of the focus group, to say what they thought the moderator wanted to hear, or to give in to an insistent, controlling respondent who demanded agreement with her point of view. And that's what my creative people were responding to or, rather, *not* responding to.

Subsequent sessions reinforced the impression. Consumers attending focus groups were highly motivated by the political dynamics of the group, their peers, and the moderator. And the politics of the situation often overrode participants' true feelings and memories of usage.

Focus groups were fine for idea generation and for picking up consumer language to use in advertising, but it became clear to me that they were not always reliable for obtaining insights into the realities of consumer usage and attitude. There had to be a better way.

Just at that time, PBS began running an unusual documentary series. A filmmaker invited himself and his camera into a family's home and lived with them for months on end, while he shot almost every incident of family life. The edited documen-

tary was not only riveting; it was also revealing of family relationships in intimate detail. Body language, facial expressions,
entrances and exits, tone of voice and word choice gave viewers
an in-depth, living portrait of that family. Most important, what
it gave was real, more real than any film or documentary about
family life I had ever seen before.

Light bulb: If it could be done for human relationships, why
not for the relationships between consumers and the products
they use? Why couldn't someone videotape the way consumers
live with products and services in their homes? Why couldn't
there be a whole new way of doing qualitative research? That
was the founding moment for Housecalls, the observational
research firm I started in 1983.

It was tough sledding at first. People are generally loathe to
abandon an accepted way of doing or looking at things, even
when the new way represents an obvious improvement. Fortunately, a former client of mine took a chance on this new kind
of qualitative research, my new company, and me. The client was
Colgate-Palmolive, and I will always be grateful to it.

Since then, the Housecalls idea has evolved into a methodology called *observational research* (also known as *ethnography*
in the marketing community). Practitioners in the marketing
community by now have employed observational research in its
various forms for almost every major product and service category. It has become one of the primary research tools for marketing, advertising, and research and development decision
makers. Housecalls now has, in addition to Colgate-Palmolive,
a broad spectrum of clients in its roster such as Duracell, Eastman-Kodak, General Mills, Hasbro, Kraft, Novartis, Ocean
Spray, Warner-Lambert, and literally dozens more.

A Word About the Origins of Observational Research

Observational research is a branch of the social science ethnography. Instead of studying cultures en masse (determining, for

example, that X percent of all seven-year-old American girls collect dolls), ethnography studies individual members of a culture in depth, closely observing the way they live and the context they live in (Melissa collects Barbie Dolls and keeps them in their unopened packages). Insights are drawn from detailed observations of people in their everyday environments.

Ethnographers originally focused on primitive tribes, living with and studying individual tribe members. Later, they began to apply the discipline to specialized urban cultures. Gradually, the methodology was applied to individuals and families in primary segments of the American population. And it wasn't long before the marketing community appropriated the observational research/ethnography to study the buying and usage habits of consumers throughout the country.

One reason for the popularity of observational research today is the contemporary need to know the consumer on a personal level. The days of mass advertising are virtually over. And with today's technology and proliferation of special-interest media, many marketers are finding they have to communicate on a consumer-by-consumer basis.

It has become imperative in today's business world to develop a reality-based, intimate knowledge of the people you want to keep as customers. There's no research tool like observational research for providing personal, up-close insight. No other research methodology allows you to burrow through your consumer's pantry, stand there while he flosses his teeth, or watch while he suffers and gets relief from an upset stomach or to be there when a new computer owner gives up trying to get it to work with her printer at one in the morning.

The rewards of observational research range from discoveries of unanticipated usage patterns to new awarenesses about product benefits and problems, from changes in lifestyle to broad strategic direction. Today many companies are turning to observational research as the first line of inquiry when considering a new product or repositioning a current brand.

This book is not a theoretical treatise. As the title says, it's an observational research handbook. The methods, the precepts, and the examples are drawn not from reference material, but from the practical, working experience of observational researchers. It's written for the marketer, the advertiser, and the research and development executive as well as the market research practitioner.

WHAT YOU WILL GET FROM THIS BOOK

Both the seasoned professional and the beginner will find *The Observational Research Handbook* useful. If you're part of management, you will learn what to expect from observational research and how to make sure your project is well conceived and carried out. We will explore the broad benefits the methodology can provide for your company, and you will learn to use some of the models as checks against your next observational research project.

The market or R&D researcher will learn how performing an observational research assignment differs from performing other kinds of qualitative research. We will explore how to set up an in-home interview and discuss what attitude to take into a respondent's personal environment, how and what to record, and what mind-set is needed to analyze and interpret the interviews. The marketing executive will discover the many ways the results of an observational research study can be used to develop new and existing products, to uncover marketing problems, and to find consumer-driven opportunities. Because they are reality-based, the discoveries made through observational research are unlikely to be made through any other form of market research.

Perhaps most importantly, this book will show how observational research can help you retain your consumers—by helping you understand how they live with your products. It will also suggest the next practical steps after your findings have been assembled.

The advertising practitioner will find a wealth of real-life communications examples that have been used in TV commercials and ads. We will explore how observational research can dig up fodder unavailable elsewhere for use in your own advertising.

While the book draws many examples from the packaged goods industry (my primary background), it will tell you how to apply observational research to any industry, including—as the techies I know assure me—software, hardware, and the Internet. The principles apply across the board. It will suggest how you can use the results to put your advertising, your marketing, your new product, and your customer retention programs on a more real basis so that they touch and motivate your consumers where they live. It also will suggest when not to use observational research and how to avoid its pitfalls.

I've found that among marketers and research and advertising people, there has always existed a breed of professionals with a special kind of hunger—to know the consumers who buy their products the way they know their wives or husbands, everything about them from the way they get up in the morning to the last thing they do at night before going to bed, and why they do what they do. Because the more they know, the better these professionals can fulfill the needs of their consumers and their companies and, not incidentally, the more successful they become.

If you're a professional who has to get as close as possible to consumers, who has to know them as intimately as possible, then observational research and this book could be exactly what you need.

WHY OBSERVATIONAL RESEARCH?

You will get closer to your consumers than ever before.

You will learn the way they buy and live with your product in their everyday lives.

You will make decisions founded on realities.

Here's a story well known to many market researchers. The management of a manufacturer of detergents wanted to find out exactly how consumers did the wash. So the manufacturer hired a research firm to videotape women consumers in their homes while they went through the whole process: sorting their clothes, putting them in the washer, adding detergent, setting the cycle, taking the clothes out of the machine and putting them in the dryer, adding a fabric softener, and finally folding up the clean clothes.

After the process, the researchers asked each woman to tell them how she determined how well the detergent had cleaned her clothes. They got the standard answers they expected: absence of stains, whites without gray, colors bright and clear. But researchers and the videotape camera happened also to pick up some very interesting behavior as each woman took the damp clothes out of the washer. Each woman smelled her clothes before putting them into the dryer.

"What was all that about?" asked the researchers, pointing out the behavior to the women. "Oh, I always do that," they answered. "Just to see if they smell clean."

"Just to see if they smell clean." From that revelation on camera, the management realized it had happened upon a whole different way of evaluating cleanliness, a way that had never been addressed, or advertised before. The result was a brand new positioning—something not easy to achieve in the detergent category. The company became the first to advertise a laundry detergent promising clean-smelling clothes. The outcome was spectacular. Consumer response to the positioning exceeded expectations.

That's a classic and very telling example of observational research in the service of marketing. It's particularly interesting because the researchers probably would not have arrived at the insight using any other form of qualitative or quantitative research.

Focus groups? Telephone interviews? Mall intercepts? Mail or Internet questionnaires? In those forms of research, consumers never would have mentioned smelling their clothes when they took them out of the washer. Because smelling one's clothes is an unconscious action, it had to be observed in everyday environments. And that's not the only kind of actionable discovery observational research can make available to market researchers and their clients.

> Most of what consumers really do and what consumers say in everyday life about the products and services they use is not accessible—except through direct observation where they live.

Observational research offers insights and opportunities not provided by other forms of market research. The methodology shines a reality-based spotlight on almost every facet of the consumer-product relationship as it actually transpires. Understanding that relationship in depth and detail—not gearing your efforts toward a single purchase—is the key to keeping your customers, the key to relationship marketing.

The practical benefits to marketers and advertisers who use observational research show up in everything from product differentiation to new product development, packaging, advertising strategy and communication, trend tracking, and even the education of company personnel. We will discuss much more about its practical uses in the next chapter. But first we need a little background: the place of observational research within the current marketing context.

THE PERSONALIZED MARKETPLACE

We live in a personalized society. We think, we act, and we buy, not en masse but as individuals with highly personal needs and wants.

You have only to turn on your TV or radio to see the evidence: a cable channel for almost every specialized interest and a radio station for practically any kind of music or talk. And, more than any other medium, the Internet is providing an opportunity for people to pursue their personal interests in depth.

Most marketers have long acknowledged the personalized marketplace. Once upon a time, they talked to the mass market. Then they discovered the niche market. Today they address the individual consumer.

You can see this evolution in marketing reflected in sophisticated databases, including records of personal preferences and personal buying habits, in E-commerce, and in personalized catalogs. And you can see it reflected on the supermarket, drugstore, and mass merchandiser shelves. The proliferation of subtly differentiated choices in a product category such as antiperspirant/deodorants or coffee boggles the mind.

Not too long ago, when you went out to buy toothpaste, your choice was among brands. You bought Colgate or Crest or Aim or any one of a dozen other brands. Today, within one brand alone, you select from an array of formulas: a whitener, baking soda, baking soda and peroxide, tartar control, plaque reduction, cavity fighting, or a combination of plaque and tartar control and cavity fighting and whitening. And would you like your toothpaste in a traditional tube, or a stand-up tube, or a pump? In a gel or a paste?

Even a function-based product like liquid dishwashing detergent is available in specialized versions: from antibacterial to sensitive skin and from formulas for pots and pans to traditional formulas. Pick the one you want.

Shopping for a computer? Log onto the Dell and Gateway websites and they'll put together a model with the exact components you need. And the same kind of choice will probably be available the next time you buy an automobile.

For much of the twentieth century, consumers had to adapt themselves and their needs to the products they found on the shelves. Today consumers have come to expect products adapted to their personal needs and wants.

Getting to Know the Individual Consumer

In the twenty-first century, in a personalized society, it's more vital than ever to know how individuals use products and services—how they live with them in their everyday personal environments, what they think about them, what place the products have in consumers' lives—and to know the *nature* of the on-going product *experience*.

- Is your consumer's liquid hand soap sitting out on the kitchen counter, or is it kept in the cabinet below the sink?

- Do your consumers take the time to enjoy the flow and feel of your hand and body lotion, or do they use it briskly as a functional, post–dish-washing reparative?

- What's the quality of relief your company's medication provides to a heartburn or athlete's foot sufferer? What makes the medication more appreciated than your competitors' remedies?

- Can families who regularly eat pasta dinners perceive a real difference between one brand and another? And is that difference the same one your advertising highlights?

- Do your single consumers plan their food shopping trips? Or do they just wing it in the supermarket aisles?

- Is your board game a part of kids' lives, or is it sitting on top of a closet shelf, under a couple of other unused games?

These are the kinds of questions that must be answered if you want to develop and maintain a reality-based relationship with your consumer, if you want to construct a marketing strategy that talks directly to their personal needs and wants, and if you want to create an advertising campaign that talks their language and connects with them emotionally. Where can the answers be found? Not in quantitative research that records purchase preferences, no matter how sophisticated the database. You will find it in the *quality* of the consumer experience.

WHAT FOCUS GROUPS DO AND DON'T DO

Early in the 1960s, qualitative research in the form of the focus group came to prominence. The focus group was the first institutionalized opportunity for advertising and marketing people to see and hear consumers revealing in depth their attitudes toward products. It soon swept the advertising and marketing community. All over the country, brand managers, account executives, and creative people eagerly spent hour after hour in small, darkened rooms behind two-way mirrors, watching consumers chat with moderators around conference tables about the products and services they used.

Focus groups were designed to reveal attitudes and insights not otherwise available. The talk, the arguments, and the ideas that came out of them were often provocative. Focus groups have generated many successful marketing strategies and advertising ideas over the years.

However, it wasn't long before the focus group began to be used and misused for everything from discovering consumer habits and practices to testing new products and exposing advertising campaigns in the works. Instead of using it to generate, people started using it to test. The consensus of the group—eight to twelve strangers trading opinions—was often taken as representative of the ideas of all consumers. Many a marketing and advertising decision involving the fate of millions of dollars and hundreds, even thousands of jobs, was made on the basis of three focus groups. And sometimes with disastrous results. The cracks in the focus group methodology became apparent in the 1980s, but it wasn't until the 1990s that people began to admit to these cracks and research people started thinking about alternatives.

In addition to the misuse of focus groups as a testing device, another problem emerged. Researchers found that focus groups revealed only consumers' *memories* of their product experiences. The memories sometimes had little to do with actual experience. They were easily colored and distorted by focus group members in the grip of peer pressure, trying to prove that their experiences, their smarts, and their status were superior to those of others in the group. Sometimes memories were altered as participants tried to please the moderator by saying what they thought she or he wanted to hear.

The advertising and marketing community was ready for a better way.

WHAT OBSERVATIONAL RESEARCH ADDS TO THE PARTY

What does observational research do that other research disciplines don't do as well? And how does it do it?

Observational research studies life—a small portion of it—closely and intensely. Think of yourself when you visit someone else's house for the first time. Your antennae are up and receiving. You're alert to every nuance of décor, every activity conducted around you, and every implication in the conversation. You register the things you take for granted in your own home or in houses you visit frequently, and you store up the new data to form your impressions of the visit.

This is what observational researchers do, except they are particularly trained to watch and record people using products in their homes or other familiar environments and then interpret the observations for marketing or product development. Every home, every consumer, and every product experience are new to them. And their antennae are working overtime. The results more often than not are fresh insights—insights highly useful to marketing, advertising, and research and development people.

The Product Experience—Not Just the Memory of It

Unlike most other forms of market research, observational research provides a window on the product experience where and when it happens. No need to rely on consumer memory, sift through filtered words or actions, or worry about focus group participants trying to look good in the eyes of others. Researchers can see and hear people using and reacting to products or services in their everyday environments.

The observational research interview takes place on the consumer's own turf, in familiar, personal surroundings, not at a facility and not in front of a dozen people, with others watching and listening behind a two-way mirror. It's much easier for respondents to relax and be themselves in familiar environments.

It is much easier for them to do what they ordinarily do and say what they really think.

The interview site is any place the consumer customarily uses the product—the bathroom, the kitchen, the car, the ball field, or the office. The interview might take place as early as 6:00 A.M. (breakfast or brushing the teeth, for example). Or as late as 10:30 P.M. (TV snacks). And in the process, the researcher might burrow through cabinets, closets, garages, and even garbage cans in search of meaningful detail. Just exploring a preteen's room, for instance, can yield a complete picture of the kid's interests, personality, and purchase habits.

Observational research usually includes in-depth questioning and probing as well as relevant action and product usage. Speech—especially articulated emotion—is part of the product experience. Interviewed consumers can tell why they do what they do with products and services. Their answers tend to be more natural and truthful when they are talking to nonjudgmental interviewers in familiar environments.

The researcher may choose to record an interview with an audio tape recorder, a still camera, or a videotape camera with or without a camera operator or just take notes. During the interview, the interviewer maintains an accepting, laid-back, anything-goes attitude—while working from the carefully thought-out interview guide. He or she cultivates a comfortable one-to-one relationship with the consumer.

A cameraperson with a minimum of equipment may also be present. If a videotape camera is used, the filming technique usually employed is what is known as *cinema verité*, developed by documentary filmmakers in France and the United States over the course of the last three or four decades. In this technique, the camera and the cameraperson become part of the furniture—unobtrusive, ignorable. Respondents forget there's a lens focused on them. And at times the cameraperson and the interviewer may even be absent, but the camera keeps rolling.

Intimate Revelations

Respondents act and talk naturally within the first few minutes of the observational research interview. It's not uncommon for respondents to reveal some of their most intimate thoughts and feelings and to do what they would usually do only in front of a close friend or relative or when they're alone:

- A middle-aged executive demonstrates how he starts swishing his morning mouthwash just before he gets into his car and then spits it out at the first stop sign. His wife comments how she hates when he does this.

- In a series of interviews with sweets consumers, a woman reveals that she hides candy in a drawer under her lingerie so her husband won't find out she indulged in the middle of the day.

- A woman who is part of a study on bathroom cleansing, admits that she cleans the family bathroom only once every three weeks.

- In the same study, after spending twenty minutes cleaning the shower tiles, a woman confesses that her husband's approval is her main motivation.

In observational research, family interaction is often free and easy. People forget the presence of the camera and the observationally trained interviewer. As the family sits around the table, plays a game, or watches television, the interviewer can choose to remain silent and observing—in effect, like a fly on the wall. Or the interviewer can become a nonintrusive part of the action, doing whatever feels comfortable and appropriate to the situation at hand. The result is often a revelation of family politics that describes who really motivates the usage or purchase decision:

- In front of a hidden camera and mike in a mass merchandiser, a mother and her young son have an argument that stops just short of hand-to-hand combat over which toothpaste to buy. You guessed it, the son gets what he wants—suggesting to the manufacturer and the retailer the strength of kids' influence in the purchase process.

FIGURE 1.1

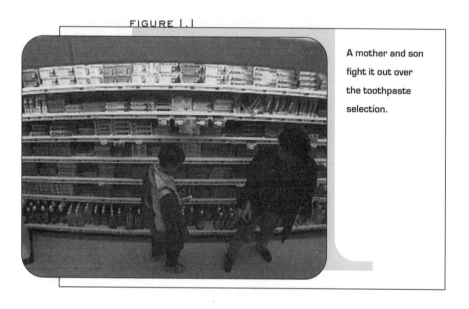

A mother and son fight it out over the toothpaste selection.

- A young husband, feeling his wife's hair after she has used a light mousse, lets his hand linger, a gesture that says worlds about the product's end benefit: a hold that is not only soft, but also clean. The dual appeal of the product to the user and to those close to her was used with significant success in consumer communication.

- An older woman snatches the deodorant her husband is trying to use to show him the right way to use it. There was no problem telling who wore the pants (and did the purchasing) in that family.

- In a gentler sequence, a whole family stands in the kitchen while the pasta cooks, each person offering to test whether it's done. This type of gathering was seen in family after family throughout the research assignment—revealing a special togetherness associated with pasta.

FIGURE 1.2

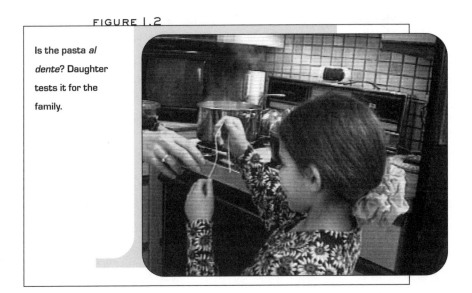

Is the pasta *al dente*? Daughter tests it for the family.

Product Differentiation

It is almost a cliché to say that most products are at parity, that there are few if any differences between one product and another in the same category—at least in the categories sold in supermarkets, drugstores, and mass merchandisers. This book espouses another point of view. While differences may be infinitesimal, or simply not exist between products, *product differences are alive and well in the consumer's head*. The consumer brings his or her own significant differentiation to the product. And observational research lets you in on the process.

Observation and depth interviewing while consumers use products in their own homes or other familiar environments provide direct access to their intimate experience. They also provide access to the context in which products have personal significance.

Small differences—real or imagined—often take on primary importance in marketing. The researcher is alert to the seemingly insignificant detail, a detail that can be highly significant in the consumer's perception—indicating a product's *perceived* key attributes and benefits. Usage-driven strategies and tactics emerge from the interviews, enabling marketers to differentiate their products and services in ways that would not have emerged through other forms of research. Here are some examples:

- Consumers were asked to cook two pastas simultaneously in their kitchens. One pasta was the consumer's regular brand, and the other pasta was a brand newly introduced to the market. A number of respondents commented that their old brand left the cooking water cloudy, while the water cooking the new brand remained clear. What did the difference mean? To some consumers it meant there was less starch in the new brand. To others, it meant that there was more actual pasta in the new brand. It was obvious that the respondents had identified in the pasta a positive attribute with a number of important benefits.

- After eating a chicken cutlet fried in cooking oil, a family member tilts the empty plate toward the researcher to show in a spontaneous demonstration the absence of oiliness—to her, a unique and important benefit.

- Observing mothers who have purchased a breakfast cereal, researchers see them dispense it to their children less often for breakfast, and more often in plastic bags as a go-anywhere snack. A change in marketing emphasis results.

- A company was marketing an extension to its line of bar soaps. Women were given the product five days before the interview and asked to use it whenever they washed their hands. When the researchers arrived for the interview, the respondents were asked to use the product again for them. As they did, they were observed taking time to work the rich lather of the reformulated bar soap into their hands. They seemed almost reluctant to rinse off the soap.

One woman volunteered her own demonstration, comparing the brand's abundant suds with the paltry suds produced by her own soap. Others attributed benefits to the lather, ranging from having extra moisturizing properties to extra value. The research led to a highly successful lather-based advertising strategy and advertising execution.

FIGURE 1.3

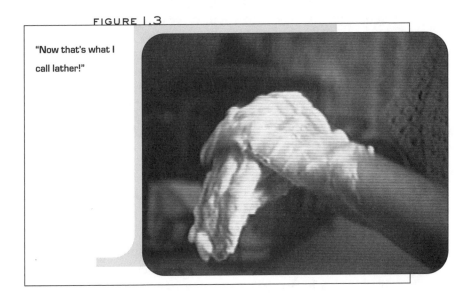

"Now that's what I call lather!"

The uses, needs, and benefits discovered by observational researchers to be most important to consumers may have nothing to do with a product's current advertising and marketing strategies. They might differ markedly from the product category's conventional wisdom. In reality, consumers may be on a very different wavelength from advertisers. Observational research can help correct the dissonance and put marketing back on the right track.

- Researchers studying athlete's foot sufferers and the way they use their medications learn that even first-time sufferers expect return bouts of the malady. Yet most medications advertise a "cure."

- A team videotaping consumers of juices and juice beverages watched them pour their beverages from the large bottles they had purchased into smaller empty water bottles—the kind with push-up tops. Consumers explained that the water bottles offered a much more convenient way to take the product with them on the jogging track, to work, or in their cars. The obvious suggestion: offer consumers a version of the product packaged like a water bottle.

- Families in a study were observed cooking and eating a food product that had been advertised to adults and primarily as a side dish. The research found that kids were the main motivators of the product purchase, and they loved it enough to consider it the main course.

- Using a hidden camera to watch shoppers select a toothbrush from a shelf in a large mass merchandiser, researchers discovered that it was almost impossible for them to find the brand they were looking for. The traditional rack system was the culprit. It almost guaranteed a jumble of undifferentiated brushes. As of this writing, a new way to stack and display toothbrushes is being developed.

New Product Development

Observational research has frequently been used to determine how consumers respond to and use new product prototypes. For instance, a company decided to market a baking soda antiperspirant/deodorant. Researchers introduced the product prototype to potential consumers in their homes, watching them use and discuss it. Respondents liked the product but could not understand the reason for the inclusion of baking soda in the formula—even though most of them used baking soda to reduce odors in their refrigerators. They couldn't make the leap between odor fighting in the fridge and odor fighting under their arms until the researcher laid out the connection for them. When she did, the camera picked up the light dawning across respondents' faces.

It became clear that to market the product successfully, it would not be enough to say "baking soda" on the package and in the advertising. Consumer communication would have to be explicit, making the connection between the odor-fighting properties of baking soda and perspiration odor. And that's exactly what the company did.

The result? The product was successfully positioned as a deodorant/antiperspirant in competition with other brands being sold as antiperspirants/deodorants.

Sometimes the product is delivered to respondents before the interview, so that they have a chance to experience it for a period of time. This might be true, for example, of a skin lotion, a new kind of software for the computer, or an over-the-counter drug requiring repeated uses. For other products, like many foods, a first impression is likely to be the lasting one. In these cases, the researcher will spring the product on respondents at the time of the interview.

The advantage of in-home testing of new products using observational research is an opportunity to start the marketing process from a reality base. This is the way consumers will actually use the product, the way they will actually respond to it, the way they will actually think about it. Instead of hit-or-miss advertising, commercials and ads can be attuned to consumer experience—emphasizing the attributes and benefits *they* think are significant. Packaging, graphics, and even the product itself can be modified right from the get-go to be of greatest use and appeal to consumers.

Observational research respondents can also help develop new products from scratch. Consumers can be highly inventive in the ways they use a particular product. Given half a chance, they'll demonstrate the problems they have with a product and then tell how to fix them. Sometimes they'll invent a small improvement, or even a whole new product right on the spot. And, most likely, their inventions will be quite practical.

Of course they're not going to reach for their drawing paper or computer and concoct a scale model right then and there. But what they will do is ask you, "Why not a deodorant shower gel?" And then tell you how useful it would be in their lives. Or, "How about a squeezing device at the end of a toothpaste tube to get out all the paste?" Or, "What about a spray top on a dish-washing detergent bottle? Hey, why don't they come that way?"

Respondents sometimes will show you instead of telling you. They'll use a fruit juice as a glaze—something you might never have thought of before. Or they'll use a baby wipe to clean up spills and stains, and you'll wonder why no one ever thought of that.

> **There is no one who knows more about what consumers want and need than consumers.**

Even if consumers don't explicitly say what they want in the way of new products or improvements, they'll point the way for you. The smart marketer will pick up the clues and move in a consumer-generated direction. There will be more about this later.

BROADER USES FOR OBSERVATIONAL RESEARCH

Studying the relationships between consumers and specific products by no means represents the limits of observational research. Observational research companies also have been called upon to provide a living portrait of various market segments. Here are a few recent examples:

- A toy company asked observational researchers to study pre-teen girls—how they spend their spare time, their favorite activities, their concerns, where they like to shop, and how they communicate with their friends. The study provided a strong basis for new product development targeting this market segment.

- Researchers studied the personal care habits of seniors—one of America's fastest-growing populations—spending hours with them as they performed some of their daily routines. They discovered among this market segment a surprising acceptance of change and responsiveness to new products.

These studies not only provided knowledge of significant market segments. They also directed marketers to consumers' unfulfilled needs and wants in a variety of product categories. The interviews became a rich mine for new product ideas, new positioning, and advertising strategies directed to each market's primary concerns.

Observational research often seeks answers to questions such as, "How do working women shop for their family's food?" Or, "What part do single-use cameras play in the lives of eighteen to twenty-four year olds?" Or, "Why do families drink less of one juice than of other juices?"

Though not a substitute for a broad, quantitative study, observational research can uncover category gaps, attitude and usage patterns, and market trends by focusing on the consumer in depth. And sometimes it is useful as a means of setting the direction and determining the areas of inquiry for a larger quantitative study.

OBSERVATIONAL RESEARCH
AND THE BOTTOM LINE

Observational research has a clear, direct impact on corporate profits in three ways: by preventing mistakes, by unearthing otherwise unavailable ideas, and by keeping companies in touch with changing consumer habits and practices.

Of all the things observational research can do, one of the most important is preventing the costly mistakes derived from erroneous assumptions. New ideas are the lifeblood of marketing, but anyone who has spent any time in the marketing community has seen new product ideas, strategies, advertising executions, promotions, and packaging go whizzing down the track powered by surface research or someone's hunch—only to run up against real-life consumer rejection. The product didn't mesh with actual consumer usage. Or the idea didn't fit into the consumer's lifestyle. Or the delivery system didn't work for the intended user.

Exposing new product and marketing ideas to the hard, clear light of consumer experience in their everyday environments offers an opportunity to see how the idea plays in reality. It may kill a pet project or crush a hunch, but if it does, it will be for the best of reasons. And it will save your company considerable amounts of money, time, and energy that might have been spent going down the wrong track.

More often than not, the job of observational research is to put you on the right track. Researchers digging into a consumer's real relationship with your product will turn up habits, practices, and consumer-generated ideas that are frequently unavailable elsewhere. They may uncover an unrealized benefit for a product that's been on the market for years, a suggestion for improving a product prototype, or a simple packaging idea no one ever thought of before. Observational research has also generated insight that motivated a new and successful strategy for a whole product category.

And sometimes observational research has identified a lifestyle intrinsically associated with a specific product, a lifestyle previously unexamined and unexploited.

No form of research is always right—particularly when it comes to generating ideas. But observational research is often on the money, because it starts with reality-based origins. Its foundation is on solid ground.

It is a cliché to say that the pace of change has increased phenomenally in American life. But it is a cliché based on truth. And nowhere is it as true as in the experience of consumers. Along with facing the incredible proliferation of choices and new products in our stores and the expansion of media options, consumers are under increasing pressure to use every minute to advantage. While the Internet is helping to create one world, the society we live in is being fragmented. In one sense, we are all living in niche markets. And the niches are getting smaller and smaller.

What's a marketer to do? There is no choice but to keep pace with change as best one can. It's vital to stay in touch with the ever-evolving consumer-product relationship *in context*. Along with the quantitative studies that provide measurement of the consumer, observational research will give you a living portrait of the consumer using (or not using) your product in everyday circumstances, in everyday life. And the wise marketer will return at regular intervals to the consumer in order to witness the changes in usage, in attitude, and in lifestyle as they relate to his or her product.

THE LIMITATIONS OF OBSERVATIONAL RESEARCH

Just as in other forms of qualitative research, there is in observational research a tendency to run with consumer reactions. But by its very nature the research is confined to a relatively small number of respondents. It explores consumers in depth, rather than en masse. Most studies range from fifteen to fifty people, so the results are not necessarily projectable to large market segments. It may not be safe to assume that observational research subjects are truly and proportionately representative of an entire market.

Thorough marketers will verify the findings of an observational study against a greater number of consumers. Or they will test the strategies and/or tactics developed from the research on their target market. Quick, inexpensive verification methods are discussed in a later chapter.

The data collected from an observational research is human and not statistical. That is its great advantage, allowing marketers to know their customer on an intimate, personal basis. But it also poses a danger. Human actions and words are open to subjective interpretation. Hearing the same responses or watching the same reactions of people, one person might think black and another white. One might see an obvious opportunity while another might see nothing at all to get excited about. There are no absolutes.

Raw observational material, whether in the form of audiotape, still pictures, or videotape, should be studied by experienced, objective observers who are trained to be careful, and to corroborate insights and conclusions with various parts of the study. They will often return to the data not just once but a number of times to check their interpretations.

That being said, it's important to assert the *reliability* of observational research. What you see and what you hear is what you get. It's real, and it reveals consumer usage and everyday attitudes with honesty and truthfulness, as long as you verify that the insights and conclusions apply to significant numbers of consumers.

What This Chapter Tells You

- As the mass market becomes individualized, you must know your consumer on a more personal basis.

- Observational research shows you how consumers actually live with your product.

- Reality-based insight into the product experience—not just the memory of it—is unavailable through other forms of research, including focus groups.

- Intimate consumer revelations in their everyday environments lead to more authentic product differentiation, new product development, and advertising executions.

- Observational research can significantly improve the profit picture.

- Observational research should be verified inexpensively against a number of consumers before the results are applied to a large market segment.

THE PRACTICAL VALUES
OF OBSERVATIONAL
RESEARCH

It can uncover a powerful, unexploited consumer benefit.

It can tell you why your current product isn't moving . . .

and test your new product in a real life context.

It can find you new consumers . . .

and help you keep the ones you've got.

A man in charge of American marketing for a multinational packaged goods company once used a word that characterized what he wanted from observational research. "I look for the *aha!*" he said. And the *aha!* or surprising insight, is the reason many people use the discipline. Even in the most mundane study—how people handle postage stamps, for instance—you can expect to learn something you didn't know before, something you would not have learned from other forms of market research. It's the reason companies come back to observational research again and again. It's also the reason more and more managers are using it as the first line of inquiry.

The insights gleaned from observational research are also sometimes the fodder and the foundation for other kinds of research a company may be planning, whether it be large telephone surveys, mall intercepts, or Internet questionnaires. Sometimes, observational research is the last research performed—a reality check before putting a marketing plan into play. And sometimes, when a company only wants to spend a limited amount on research and is more interested in depth than breadth of insight, observational research might be the first and only line of inquiry.

How does observational research feed into the marketing process? What are the values it can offer those responsible for the health and well-being of a brand?

A Case in Point

A classic example of observational research in use occurred when a large food processor was experiencing flat sales of a key line extension. The item was a packaged convenience food, positioned as a side dish for the whole family.

All the taste tests had been positive. The quality was clearly better than anything else in its category. And it was easy and convenient to prepare. Although priced slightly higher than its competitors, it was well within the cost range of other side dishes. By all measures, the probability of purchase was high. The product was destined to be the big winner in its category.

So what happened? After a year in the marketplace, why were consumers coming back to the brand only once in a while? Why wasn't it a regular presence at the dinner table? What was standing in the way of the high-flying success everyone anticipated? The company came to an observational research firm to get a handle on the reasons.

Researchers visited the homes of consumers who were currently using the brand, at dinner and at lunch. They watched while consumers prepared the product, while family members ate it, and while the plates and pots were washed afterward. The consumers being observed were not new purchasers of the category or the brand name. Most respondents had enjoyed the original product in the line for many previous years.

Researchers saw adults cooking hamburgers or chicken together with the new line extension. They observed them serving the line extension alongside a meat dish—sometimes in a separate dish and sometimes on the same plate with a vegetable or salad. And they watched while the family dug in. But a funny thing happened on the way to the mouth. While the adults and children of the family ate the meal the way the chef intended— a bite of meat, a bite of the side dish, with occasional forays into the vegetable or salad—the teenagers attacked their food differently. Not only did they eat the side dish first, but they actually finished it and went back for seconds even before half the meat on their plates was gone.

Observing the order of eating and the gusto teenagers brought to the side dish early in the study, researchers decided to ask subsequent teenage respondents a simple question. Did they consider the side dish a side dish or was it the main course? No question about it. For teenagers, the company's line extension was the main course of the meal. And not just for dinner. When they were home during the day, teens often chose this product as their main lunch food and sometimes even as a snack.

When the interviews had been completed and analyzed, the research company made the obvious suggestion to the food processor. Corroborate the evidence, but consider repositioning the line extension as a main course for kids, with emphasis on teenagers. If their observations projected, such a change in strategy might accomplish two positive goals. First, the product would be directed to consumers who ate it most often. Second, if positioned as a main course, the product would be removed from the overly competitive world of other side dishes: rice, potatoes, and pastas of all kinds.

The client had many questions. Its main concern was that such a strategy might be too narrow in scope. It would be a radical repositioning for the line extension. The other products in the line were doing very well as all-family side dishes.

Fortunately, the company had recently completed a quantitative end-user study on all the products in the line. They decided to go back and take another look at the numbers for this line extension. And there it was: The product skewed higher among families with teenagers. They bought more of it, and they bought it more often. The evidence had been sitting right under the company's nose all the time.

The next step was a concept test. In a series of mall intercepts and focus groups, simple concept boards embodying the new strategy were shown separately to teenagers and their mothers. The respondents included those who had previously used the line extension and those who were consumers of other products in the line and/or the category.

The response to the concepts was positive, emboldening the company to direct its advertising agency to create two different campaigns—one directed to mothers and the other to kids. Following a creative exploratory, stealomatic representative commercials were developed. (A *stealomatic* is an inexpensive way of producing commercials for testing. It uses visuals from previously produced commercials.) The commercials directed to moms showed the whole family eating the product but featured teenagers going back for seconds. The commercials directed to kids featured the product as the favorite main course of teenagers.

The commercials were exposed to potential consumers through an advertising testing service. They tested well.

In previous years, even with the good scores the commercials achieved, the food processor might have taken the time to put the campaign into a test market as the next step. But with today's highly competitive grocery shelf and the fast pace of the packaged goods business and because enough evidence had accumulated to support the new strategy, the campaign was deemed ready for national exposure. Full-blown versions of the commercials were produced and put on television.

The results? As of this writing, although it's too early to project very far into the future, there has been a clear uptick in sales. And it looks like the product has finally broken from its plateau.

What was the role of observational research in this marketing effort? What did it do that other kinds of research didn't do or couldn't have done? It illuminated a consumer usage pattern that was already there in the numbers but that hadn't been noticed. It literally brought the teenage predilection for the product as a main course to life for the company. The research articulated an unexploited consumer relationship to the product that led to a new and productive marketing effort.

Perhaps some perspicacious marketer poring over the quantitative study might have stumbled upon the same answer one day. But it hadn't happened yet. It took observational research to find and show the pattern and to make it possible for decision makers at the food processor and its agency to turn the pattern into action.

Although this is a classic example of observational research at work, companies employ close observation of their consumers for many purposes. Despite the many uses of the research, however, there is one way to determine its effectiveness. And that is change. Change is the underlying objective of any market research: Change in the product, change in the package, change in the strategy, change in the advertising, change in the promotion, change in the pricing, change in the company's perception of the consumer, and, most importantly, change in the consumer's relationship to the product. Why do the research unless it leads to action? Research projects are too expensive to serve merely as confirmation of what you already know.

Let's examine some of the other ways companies use observational research to make positive changes in their marketing efforts.

UNCOVERING MEANINGFUL BENEFITS

Most marketing people would agree that, while many factors are important in a product's success or failure in the marketplace, meaningful consumer benefits are the core reason. Beyond price, packaging, shelf position, and promotion, a product lives or dies because of what the consumer perceives it does or doesn't do for him or her in everyday life. The benefit may be purely functional—for example, when the product is a remedy for athlete's foot. Or the benefit may involve a broad lifestyle appeal when the product is a car or high-priced item of clothing.

Broadly speaking, there are two ways of finding the right benefits to feature in the marketing of almost any product or service. They are not necessarily mutually exclusive. One way is to list all the potential benefits and allow consumers to choose which have the most appeal. A series of concepts embodying potential benefits is presented to consumers via mall intercepts or focus groups, and they are asked to react to each one. This is the method most often chosen in the past. Unfortunately, the method restricts itself to those benefits perceived by the marketing or research people making up the list.

The other way is to discover benefits in the consumer's product experience. Observational research can be very useful in producing reliable results through this approach.

Often, the process of discovery begins with the interviewer noticing a consumer's reliance on a specific attribute or physical aspect of a product. Studying the consumer ideas about comfort for a central air-conditioning manufacturer, an observational researcher visited homes in which the product had been installed. When the researcher asked to see the unit, respondents did not take them first to the air conditioner. Instead, respondents took them to the machine's control panel, explaining all the things it could do, from automatically turning on and off at programmed times to offering separate room programming. It also seemed very important for consumers to describe how strategically placed the control panel was.

Following her fine-tuned instincts, the researcher began to probe the whole issue of control—first in terms of internal climate control. The best climate control was total control. And then beyond control of air conditioning, consumers sought control in the areas of home security, insurance, and even financial security. It soon became apparent that, among these upper middle–class respondents, for air conditioning as for other aspects of their lives, the more control, the more comfort. It was not so important how well the air conditioning cooled, but how well the consumer could control it. This discovery was highly useful for strategic thinking and one that began with a physical control panel.

A story that is outside the realm of marketing but that uses classic observational insight illustrates how an observant pair of eyes, watching the way people relate to a product attribute, can detect a problem leading to a benefit that will change consumers' lives. An American stationed briefly in a remote Asian village noticed that most of the men in the village were permanently bent over and in pain by the time they were thirty. Watching them in their fields, he saw that the hoes they traditionally used had two-foot long handles, forcing them almost to double over as they worked the soil. Obviously, here was the cause of their back problems.

He sent away for a bunch of long-handled hoes. It took a week or so of going out into the fields and working the soil himself before the American was able to get just one of the village farmers to try the newfangled hoe. But the rest of the village noticed how the farmer was able to stand up straight as he farmed.

Before the American was reassigned, the whole village had started to use the long-handled hoes, and the men had begun to straighten up and walk without pain for the first time. The new hoes changed their lives. Observational research may not always lead to such a dramatic change, but the benefits it uncovers can lead to significant product differentiation.

Watching consumers use one of the major brands of baby wipes on their infants' bottoms, researchers noticed that they employed only one or two baby wipes before putting on a fresh diaper. Questioned about whether they often used the same number, most consumers said they needed fewer baby wipes from this brand to get their kids completely clean than they did when using other brands. The result was that less time was needed for this messy chore and less time was available for baby to squirm and get cranky. At changing time the baby was happier.

Why fewer wipes? Because consumers thought that the product, bearing a very well-known brand name, was made with better paper. It so happened that this particular baby wipe was made with paper equivalent to and no better than that of other brands. It was the brand name that triggered attribute perceptions and gave rise to the benefit. The benefit was determined through the researcher's observations. The issue might never have arisen in other forms of research.

In another study, researchers attended a series of parties at which an instant camera was in use. In each case, before the camera was brought out and people began to take pictures, the party consisted mostly of one-on-one conversations. The act of taking pictures and showing the photos almost immediately brought the party together. People clustered around the photographer to see what they and their friends looked like. They became more animated. Laughter and talk filled the room. The party came to life. A clear end benefit was seen by the reviewer: The camera helped make living more fun.

What's Wrong with This Product?

Sometimes the fault in a problem brand does not lie in the strategy, the positioning, or the way the benefits are communicated to the consumer. Sometimes the problem is something about the product itself—perhaps a little glitch not noticed by R&D, not mentioned in a quantitative survey, or not discussed in a focus group. Sometimes you have to be right there, while consumers are using the product, to discover a problem.

Observers watching users of a certain brand of computer heard more than the ordinary share of expletives as the screen suddenly shifted from the material users were working on to rows of icons. No, they hadn't wanted to go back to the desktop, thank you. But you just couldn't help hitting those darned Windows keys, one right under the shift key and the other near the forward slash, when you didn't mean to. And, yes, you could go right back to your material, but it was a pain being interrupted in the middle of a thought. What did you need the keys for anyway? And why not have just one Windows key if you're going to have any? And why not put it in a slightly out-of-the-way location? As is, those keys served more as reminders of Microsoft's omniscient presence than of anything else.

Even the sharpest R&D people working for the smartest companies, like the rest of us, sometimes think and breathe in a narrow world. And even with all the discussions and testing and diligence, it's quite possible for them, along with those responsible for marketing the product, to overlook an annoyance that could help a product underachieve its sales goals.

A food company thought it had a winner with crisp, firm chunks of graham-flavored cereal. The prototype tasted great and kept its shape and firmness in milk, and the kids they tested it on loved it.

But there was one little problem. They had tested the product on kids over eight years old who literally ate it up. The researchers had never seen such enthusiasm. So they put the new product in a couple of test markets. It took observational research to discover (unfortunately after the fact) that many of the kids *under* eight had a hard time getting their mouths around the chunks. And they had a harder time biting down on them. They were too oversized for the undersized.

A large manufacturer of floor coverings had another kind of problem. In the retail outlets where the company's tiles and other coverings were sold, there were literally hundreds of different styles, patterns, colors, and textures of the manufacturer's products available and on display. Yet the people who bought floor covering for their homes were frequently ignorant of brand. In fact, even some home owners who had recently purchased one

FIGURE 2.1

Observational research shows this cereal is too big for a little mouth.

of the manufacturer's products and were living with it had no idea who the manufacturer was. Their choices were made on the advice of the salesperson, their installer or building contractor, or a friend.

Why was there such minor brand registration? Why did consumers place so little importance on brand name? Observational research turned up one of the main reasons. Consumers selected by multiple criteria—style, color, material, and price. And there were actually so many selections in each category at the floor covering stores that people felt confused, fatigued, and incapable of making any kind of an informed choice. Brand was the last thing on their minds.

The recommended solution was that the manufacturer associate the brand with easier selection. The company should employ contemporary technology to create an easy, simple guide for consumers to use even before they started looking through the tiles. The styles, colors, materials, and prices would be categorized in accordance with the most common needs (by kind of room, for example), and the selections would be instantly viewable. The manufacturer should make the process so simple that consumers would only have to ask the salesclerk for a specific style number that they had viewed in the brand selection device just a few moments after walking into the store. The system was much better not only for the consumer but for the retailer as well, whose salespeople would have to spend less time with each customer.

Observational research can identify even the smallest problems that might inhibit the purchase decision. In the process of studying the oral care habits and practices of senior citizens, a researcher introduced a new toothbrush to respondents and asked them to try it. Within a few minutes, it was evident that a number of respondents felt a slight but vague antipathy toward the product. For some reason, they didn't think it was their kind of toothbrush.

Reviewing the videotapes, the reason soon became clear. Seniors were having difficulty opening the plastic package encasing the new brush. It took a bit of effort and patience. Turning up the sound volume on the videotaped interviews, one respon-

FIGURE 2.2

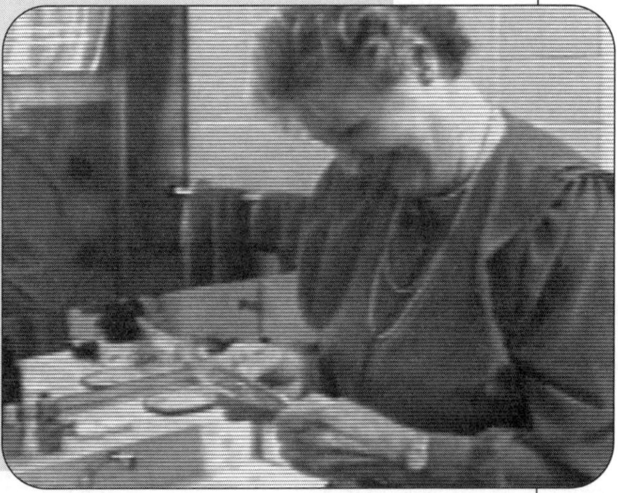

A toothbrush manufacturer discovers that seniors have trouble opening the package.

dent was heard to mutter under her breath, "This brush is for younger people." Obviously, their first contact with the product—the package—had a radical effect upon their perceptions of it. This simple problem was simply fixed—thanks to close observation.

If there are practical, in-use product glitches, observational research will usually bring them to light as no other form of research can do.

FINDING NEEDS
CONSUMERS DON'T EXPRESS

In almost any product category, there are gaps—unfulfilled needs and wants—seldom expressed by consumers. Observational research can reveal those gaps.

Here's a simple example. Observational researchers riding in consumers' cars as they consumed a common beverage noticed that drivers who bought anything but the smallest size bottle kept it in their hands or wedged it between the seat belt and the gear box. A researcher happened to see one person's beverage spill when the car hit a bump. The problem for consumers was that the larger bottles did not fit into vehicle cup holders. The holder was made for a smaller container. The solution was to develop longer, narrower bottles or taper the ends.

Women using a hair gel were seen to wipe their hands with a towel after each application before picking up their comb or brush. Questioned about it, they said that the gel left their hands sticky. They explained that they thought of the stickiness as a necessary part of the gel experience if they wanted to keep their hair in place. But stickiness wasn't necessary at all. A less sticky gel was feasible. Queried about its potential appeal, gel users all responded positively.

Anthropologists and observational researchers have noticed that the family computer is now the equivalent of the family hearth. Family members use it on their own at different times of the day, and they use it together to play electronic games, to communicate with distant friends and relatives, and to find mutually interesting information. With this insight, companies can develop a host of products related to the computer *experience*, just as they responded to television with related products such as TV dinners and snacks, TV *Guide*, and soap opera magazines.

Finding areas for new product development is a matter of keeping one's eyes and ears open during research and while studying the completed interview. There is no product that completely fulfills every need and every want for every consumer. There is always a gap, however small it may seem at first.

It is helpful to focus on analogous categories as you work. For instance, on both a functional and a psychological level, a boy's bicycle is his car. Thinking of cars while thinking about bicycles enables you to conceive of peripheral bike products resembling real automobile accessories. Or seeing the way consumers use the local Moviephone service might give some retailers the idea to use similar technology to offer his or her goods to customers.

TESTING NEW PRODUCTS FOR REAL

Broadly speaking, new products in the past were usually tested either by bringing potential consumers to a facility where they were watched as they ate, drank, used, or applied the product or by giving them a prototype and asking them to respond to an inquiry after using it. Both methods have value, but both miss something. Watching consumers relate to the product in a facility lets you in on their intimate responses and reactions, but it tells you nothing about what happens when consumers actually live with a product and make it part of their lives. Sending them a prototype and asking for a written summary of their reactions after living with it is more realistic. But a questionnaire is just a questionnaire, and it provides only an abstract picture of the relationship between product and consumer—without the spontaneous reactions that bring the relationship to life and that so often produce exciting marketing insights and ideas.

In recent years, various companies have begun to supplement or substitute their new product-testing methodologies with in-home observational research. For some companies, in-home observation begins at a very early stage of product development, before the package or graphics have been conceived and before options such as flavor, application system, or program configuration have been locked in.

If the new product is one that has a cumulative effect (skin lotion, certain medications, and home fitness equipment, for example), the respondent is given the prototype and asked to use it for a number of days. At the end of the period, when enough time has passed to establish a pattern and to achieve whatever effect the product promises, observational researchers visit the respondents to watch closely as they use the product once again.

Much can be learned from such observations. The older product-testing methodologies may disclose the potential consumer's overall satisfaction or dissatisfaction with the product. But observational research also will tell you and show you why.

Are consumers having trouble accessing your new Internet site? Observational research will show you the icons consumers select, how long before they arrive at the information they're looking for, and the level of frustration they experience.

Are consumers loving the new hand and body lotion you just formulated? Observational research will show you the lingering touch of a woman's hand as she smooths your product on her legs, and the soft, relaxed look on her face. And you might hear how she's begun to use your lotion as part of her time out from obligation and pressure—for a mini spa.

Got a new flavor of jam for your line? Observational research will show you if your product is out on the breakfast table in the morning, who in the family spreads it on toast, and

FIGURE 2.3

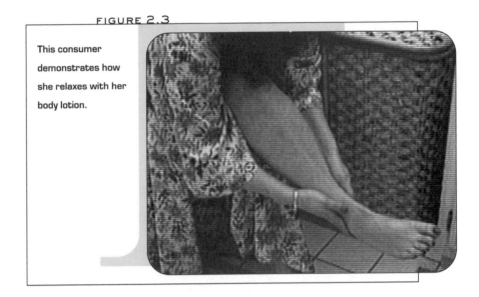

This consumer demonstrates how she relaxes with her body lotion.

where it's kept when breakfast is over. And you'll get the authentic reactions of all family members.

You may not want to use observational research as the *only* method of product testing, but you will certainly want to use it at least in conjunction with more traditional methodologies. Observational research is a reality check on your new product ideas. Will your hot new prototype really be as significant in potential consumers' lives as you think it will be? Have all the problems truly been ironed out? Are there any surprises, positive or negative, you should be prepared for once it hits the marketplace? Observational research will tell you and show you.

A food company once had an idea: Interesting food entrées sold in upscale supermarkets could compete with gourmet food stores then offering gourmet entrées at higher prices in major urban centers. The observational researchers hired to understand the product's usage watched upscale consumers in major cities prepare the prototype and react well to the taste and the idea. Respondents pegged the product somewhere between Lean Cuisine and gourmet. At the price point the company originally set, all was well and good. Consumers could see a definite place for the new entrées among their meal options, and most felt they'd be getting good value for their money.

But at some point the food processor started thinking about the product as a truly gourmet entrée—on a par with the entrées available at boutique gourmet take-out stores. Despite the research company's closely documented admonitions to the contrary, the food processor raised the price, promoted the product as a gourmet entrée now available in the supermarket, and prepared to reap the profits. What the company reaped was more like a hatful of rain. The potential consumer was simply unwilling to pay the same price for a supermarket entrée as for an entrée available at a gourmet food store. The brand died, but might have gone on to a solid niche success if the company had heeded the observational research.

On a more positive note, when hair mousses were about to be introduced in the United States, a company preparing to distribute a brand that had achieved some success in Europe asked an observational research company to explore American women's reactions to the product. The hair mousse was tested with potential consumers. After trying it for a couple of weeks, consumers were interviewed in their homes as they used the product once again.

The in-use reactions to the mousse were highly encouraging and not only because of the level of enthusiasm. The women who had been using it demonstrated benefits of all kinds for the researchers. They showed how the product disappeared instantly into the hair and how it held the hair softly without stiffness or stickiness. One young woman asked her husband to run his fingers through her hair and tell the researchers what he felt. "Nothing," he said, which is exactly what the company wanted to hear.

Another woman invented her own demonstration to show that the mousse also worked as a conditioner. After shampooing, she used the mousse on one side of her hair and not on the other. Then she tried to run her fingers through her hair. On the side where she hadn't used the mousse, her fingers got stuck—held by the unconditioned strands. But on the side where she had used the mousse, her fingers easily passed through.

FIGURE 2.4

This woman invented
her own mousse
demonstration.

Ultimately, the brand was positioned as the mousse that not only holds without leaving your hair stiff or sticky, but that conditions your hair as well. This position, derived directly from the observational research, helped the product achieve success.

The newness that you expose to observational research need not move the earth. Not every product advance is a revolution. It can be as simple as a new kind of opening for a package, a new flavor line extension, or a small modification to a software program. With improvements of this kind, what you want to know first is whether consumers notice the change, and then if the change or improvement was helpful in consumers' everyday lives.

DISCOVERING NEW MARKETS

We express who we are or think we are or who we would like to be in various ways: the way we act toward others, how we talk, how we hold ourselves, the neighborhood we choose to live in, what we wear, and in many other aspects of our daily lives. And one of the significant ways we identify ourselves is through our choices of products.

The analgesic consumers use for their headaches often indicates the generation they belong to. Those who use Bufferin are often older than consumers who use Excedrin who are usually older than those who use Tylenol who are probably older than Advil consumers.

There is a style and personality difference, as Malcolm Gladwell pointed out in the March 22, 1999, issue of *The New Yorker*, between women who use Clairol and those who use L'Oreal to color their hair. And experienced professionals can tell the difference just by the way the women dress and talk without even looking at their hair.

Consumers who keep supplies of eggs, bacon, or oatmeal for breakfast are likely to lead different lives from those whose pantries contain Pop Tarts and Special K. And those who use Macintosh computers in their homes aren't using them for only functional reasons. In their minds, a Mac differentiates them from the more buttoned-down PC user. (Think what they will, this book was written on a PC.)

These idiosyncrasies should not be treated isolated phenomena. No matter what kind of product you may be marketing, it pays to look at related and some unrelated product categories within the consumer's everyday environment. Each category and each brand your respondent buys, including the sizes and the variations, provides a well-marked road map of his or her life. And there is no better way to read the map than to use observational research. If you know what's in the fridge, the pantry, the medicine cabinet, the garage, and the closets, you can write a pretty accurate biography and description of that family's life.

And you can talk directly to their interests and concerns in every piece of communication, from the package to the advertising to the promotion to the Web site. Moreover, what you may be able to do once you have this information is to discover a whole new market for your product or a new way of defining your mainstream consumer.

Researchers who were present when families sat down to eat dinner prepared from an inexpensive packaged entrée observed that a number of these families said grace before the meal. They also noticed that, like the entrée they were eating, the brands in their pantries and refrigerators tended to be the long-established standbys—Kraft Cheese, Blue Bonnet Margarine, Mazola Cooking Oil, Kellogg's Corn Flakes, Birdseye Frozen Peas. Had the observational researchers also looked at their cleaning supplies, no doubt they would have found brands like Tide, Mr. Clean, and Lysol. The road map clearly said conservative, family values, long-term commitments. This definition of their market proved to be true for many purchasers of the product and guided future consumer communication.

In another series of interviews in which the product studied was pasta sauce, it was observed that those who tended to buy premium brands often had many cookbooks gathering dust in their homes. Researchers also noticed that the side dishes, appetizers, and condiments in their refrigerators were frequently bought from specialty stores rather than supermarkets. They may not have had time to cook from scratch any longer, but it was important to them to be able to *individualize* the family's dinner—to make it their own creation even when it came out of a box, can, or jar. Whether that consumer group is large or small, it represents an interesting opportunity for the right marketer to develop a line of premium, easy-to-prepare specialty foods that might even lure this kind of consumer to purchase them in the supermarket, were they marketed there.

It pays to recruit some respondents from outside the mainstream. If you stick to the kind of consumer who usually buys your product, you may be missing some connections with different users who might comprise a sizable subgroup. Even when your product is used mostly by twenty-year-old working women, you just might want to include a few older, nonworking users to see if there are differences in the ways your product fits into their lives.

Observational research, by the discoveries it makes in the process of exploring the lives of respondents, can find the connections that create new markets and new consumers for your company.

Keeping Your Current Consumers

It is a marketing cliché to say that consumer retention is even more important today than is gaining new consumers. For one thing, it's a lot cheaper to hold on to a consumer than to convince someone loyal to another brand to come into your fold. Once you lose a consumer, it's even more difficult to get him or her back.

Perhaps the greatest single value of observational research is that it provides you with the kind of knowledge you need to secure a relationship with your consumer: an intimate knowledge of the way your consumer actually lives with your product—not in the abstract, not by the numbers, but up close and personal.

Once you've completed an observational study, you will know the consumers as if you stood in their homes yourself and watched and chatted with them as they used your product. You will know what they like and don't like about your brand in depth and detail, how they store it, how they handle it, how they use it, and how they dispose of it. You will understand—in realistic, day-to-day terms—the place and value of your product in their lives in a way that no other kind of research can reveal. You will know what makes the consumer your consumer.

The discoveries you make through observational research will enable you to develop or modify your communication, your package, and your product to fit precisely into your consumers' lives. You will enjoy a relationship based on your knowledge and their trust. You will truly understand who they are and what they want.

In today's changing marketplace, in which your consumer is subject to so many pulls and pressures, it pays to perform an observational research study at regular intervals. Increased competitive activity and economic vicissitudes, among other factors, can strongly influence your consumer–product relationship, and you will want to know how on an ongoing basis.

Hunting for Advertising Fodder

One of the most productive uses of observational research is in finding strategic and execution ideas for advertising. Nothing resonates among consumers exposed to commercials, print ads, and Internet banners as well as their own product applications, ideas, and language. Seeing themselves in a piece of advertising confirms on many levels that this product is for them.

A team charged with developing advertising for a large chain of amusement parks featuring awesome roller coasters knew that its audience would be teens and adults in their early twenties. What they didn't know was the exact nature of the fun these people had on the roller coaster. Was it the feeling of being safely scared, their own sense of personal courage, the thrill of speed?

Three members of the team—a creative person, an account representative, and a researcher—decided to visit one of the nearby amusement parks in the chain and find out for themselves. They rode the roller coaster, watching while teenagers all around them squealed and cringed in anticipation as the cars slowly climbed the towering hills and then whizzed at breakneck speed down the other side. They listened to the shouts, the screams, and the laughter. But nothing was coming through.

Nothing other than the typical noises and postures seen in a hundred different commercials and ads for amusement parks.

It was only when the roller coaster stopped and everyone began to get off that the team members realized what the experience had been to these teenagers. They were giving each other high fives and patting each other on the back. They had lived through a scary few minutes in each other's company—it was a little like being in a battle together—and they had come through. This bonding experience was a major part of the thrill, the end benefit of the roller coaster for these teenagers, a benefit that could easily be expressed in visuals and words in the advertising for the amusement park chain.

Observers of regular consumers of baked, low-fat potato chips reacting to old-fashioned high cholesterol chips were amazed. Some consumers went into paroxysms of rapture the instant the rich, high-fat scent of those old-fashioned chips hit their nostrils. The smell released childhood memories of the days when chips were just chips. Consumers remembered family picnics at the shore, sitting in front of the TV with friends and munching through a whole bag without care, and summer barbecues in the backyard, when the sun went down just as they finished the last chip buried on their plates under a hamburger roll.

The same scent might not be there when consumers open a bag of low-fat baked chips. Nevertheless, consumer memories could be associated with the low-fat product and used as evocative emotional settings in the advertising.

More than a consumer's rational comments or step-by-step usage of a product, what is often most valuable in observational research is the emotional response to a product or a problem. The emotional factor is what makes people watching a commercial connect to a product. Observational research frequently finds that response on the home turf of consumers, where they can react naturally. The researcher may see it in an explosion of anger or in a sudden burst of nostalgia, as in the potato chip experience. Emotions can also be picked up in subtle body language—the slight wrinkling of the nose, the slanted posture, the way a consumer handles a product, the hesitation before putting a forkful into the mouth.

> The telling gesture and the cut-through phrase are the stuff of great ads and commercials, and they are found where they happen—in the consumer's everyday environment.

Observational research can also make connections between seemingly disparate actions—connections highly useful in advertising. You'll see later how observational research discovered a relationship between heartburn and stress and how the discomfort produced by heartburn can upset personal and family equilibrium. Another connection discovered by observation was between crisp, freshly laundered clothes and feelings of self-worth. People putting on perfectly clean and pressed clothes in the morning tended to leave the house feeling up about themselves and ready to meet others in the course of the day. This discovery, made after interviewing men and women as they left for work in the morning, led to a new detergent campaign promising users they would "Start the day fresh."

Words uttered only with the greatest reluctance in front of peers in a focus group often come out readily in the course of observational research. Respondents in their own homes or cars feel less inhibited than they do in front of strangers in a facility. And language picked up in everyday environments and used in advertising usually has authentic resonance with consumer audiences.

There are observational researchers whose sole job it is to work the streets where teenagers congregate and pick up the latest synonyms for *cool* or *good looking* or *exciting*. Language researched this way is particularly useful in soft drink, snack, and music advertising addressed to young people. But if you're going to use the latest phrases, you had better stay on the streets and keep your ears open. The most popular words and phrases can change from month to month.

Special gestures or idiosyncratic actions are frequently even more memorable than special language. We live in a visual culture. We may forget what Michael Jordan said at his last news conference, but we will always remember his high, elegant leaps above the basket, embodying our dreams of grace and glory, to score another two points for the Bulls. The resonance of visual images applies as well to advertising. The gesture, the action that represents something in all of us, pulls us in and helps us identify with the product.

Anyone who does the household laundry will identify with a woman who pulls the family's clothes out of the dryer and smells the fresh, just-washed scent. A man with athlete's foot who rubs one boot on top of the other to relieve the itch will get a head nod from anyone who has had the condition. A kid putting his potato chips inside his sandwich so it's crunchier will capture the attention of potato chip lovers. A woman who can't stop making lather with a soap until her hands are gloved with it says volumes about how the soap feels on your hands. All these actions were picked up by observational research and used in advertising.

What the researcher should look for and record is the special memorable gesture—perhaps a bit unconventional but highly indicative of a benefit or a problem. It's one thing for people to demonstrate clean, freshly brushed teeth by smiling. There is nothing especially new or indicative there. But one successful toothpaste campaign some years ago showed users licking their teeth to show how clean and smooth they *felt*.

More recently, a campaign for a hemorrhoid remedy created instant identification with sufferers by showing men and women squirming while seated at various public events, shifting from one position to another and finding no position comfortable.

Real-life visuals that work in advertising are not always easy to find, but when they are found, they are almost always effective. The observational researcher can be of enormous help in finding them.

More often than not, advertising campaigns feature ideal settings for the people who use products in ads and commercials. But there are many instances when a more real setting is appropriate, when the gory details enhance consumer identification. Commercials that depict lifestyle problems such as not having enough time or being too much in demand or having too much to clean often show the problems in their worst but recognizable light. The same frequently goes for some physical problems such as headaches. Observational research can help by recording not only the way real consumers actually experience such problems, but also *where* they experience the problems, such as a dark, rainy street, a messy house, or a stalled commuter train.

When the researcher is hunting for advertising fodder, sometimes it's appropriate to take along one of the creative people working on the brand, particularly if the research is being conducted sans videotape. There's nothing like the *pow!* that happens when a copywriter or art director sees a potential visual right as it's happening or hears a set of memorable words spoken by a real consumer in response to a product used in a real environment. There is one caveat: The creative people should not talk to the consumer. They're along strictly to exercise their advertising antennae. If they've got a question for the consumer, they can tell the researcher. The worst thing that could happen is for too many voices to interrupt the intimacy and the flow of the interview.

Later, we'll explore what to do with the findings of observational research once they've been assembled. But first, let's talk about how to make sure you get the most from your next observational research project.

WHAT THIS CHAPTER TELLS YOU

- Observational research provides findings that can easily be turned into action—undiscovered consumer needs and benefits directly exploitable in marketing and advertising efforts.

- Observational research will help you form a relationship instead of just a transaction with your consumer, a relationship that encourages ongoing purchase and usage of your product.

- You'll watch consumers come up with reality-based uses and vivid, advertiseable language as they try out new products in their homes.

- Observational research can find and bind together consumers' personal idiosyncrasies to form a whole new market segment.

- Observational research can find in-use product problems that elude even R&D.

OBSERVATIONAL TECHNIQUES

With team observation, your people go along.

Still camera and audiotape are the anthropologist's way.

The videotape camera and the depth interview catch body and verbal language.

Giving the camera to respondents gets you close to the in-group.

Direct observation of people in their everyday environments, a branch of ethnography, has evolved from the days when anthropologists such as Ruth Benedict or Margaret Mead would visit a remote society and stay for months on end, taking notes and perhaps making a few sketches. As direct observation began to be applied to American society and specifically to results-driven market research, various practical ethnographic techniques were developed to fit commercial needs.

Today, you have a choice of four primary techniques:

- Team observation
- Still camera and audiotape

- Videotape

- Combined technique

Each of these techniques has advantages and disadvantages, and the choice among them is often made on the basis of the comfort level felt by the company paying for the research. Who needs to be involved? To whom will the findings be presented? How will the research be used? These questions should be answered before selecting a specific technique.

What Is Common to All Techniques

Direct observation is an opportunity to discover the place of a product or service in the lives of consumers—how it fits into the texture of their everyday experience. Researchers will pore over the kitchen cabinet and the refrigerator, the medicine chest, the laundry room, the garage, or the CD-ROMs stacked near the computer, examining each relevant product and utensil.

Researchers don't stop with observation. They want to know why the consumers they interview do what they do. Each respondent is questioned, often in minute detail, about the reasons for purchasing a product and for storing it and using it in a particular way and about its relationship to other products and services. Questions may be directed to just one respondent or to the whole family. Consumers are questioned while they shop the aisles of a supermarket, drugstore, or mass merchandiser.

Here is one woman's breathless answer to why and when she would buy a new prepared, packaged dinner entrée she had just experienced as a prototype. It's the kind of detailed, individual revelation usually not forthcoming from focus groups, and it characterizes exactly the consumer's potential relationship to the product:

> *I'm up at 7:00, making the breakfast at 7:15, getting the two boys out to the 7:33 train, coming back and getting*

Christopher ready to go to school at 8:15, taking the dog for a walk, at 8:30 getting in my car, arriving at the school where I teach at 8:40, teaching until 11:30, coming back for Christopher's lunch from 11:40 to 12:15, getting back in the car and going back to my job from 12:15 till 3:00, getting back in the car at 3:00 and picking up my son, Christopher, going to the station and picking up my other son, going to the orthodontist with that son, coming back and picking my third son up from soccer practice, and then realizing I forgot to take meat out of the freezer at 7:30 in the morning. That's when I would stop at the Pelham Gourmet and pick up something like this.

In-depth observation and interviewing will provide first-hand, reality-based insights into the consumer experience, insights that often differ from those provided by hearsay or memory-based research. Here are just a few of the issues having a direct bearing on marketing and advertising strategy that an observational visit might reliably illuminate:

- What are the consumer's dominant values?

- How does the product enhance (or not enhance) the consumer's lifestyle?

- How does the consumer's lifestyle modify the product's purchase pattern?

- Who in the family actually uses the product? Who consumes it?

- How do they use the product? Do they follow directions or do they develop their own special usage patterns?

- What sense is most involved in the product experience? Touch? Taste? Sight? Hearing? Smell? What is the quality of that experience?

- Do any problems show up in use? How significant are they to the consumer?

- What product attributes and benefits are observed to be most important? Do they differ from those advertised?

- Is the product kept along with utility or indulgence products?

- Is it kept out in front or in the back of the cabinet or drawer?

- How much of the product has been used? Has a new package already been purchased?

- What other products on hand are sometimes used instead?

- Do parents monitor family usage? Do the kids comply?

- How does the family refer to the product in everyday conversation—generically or by brand name?

Each of these questions has a direct bearing on marketing strategy and consumer communication. And all four observational techniques provide specific, authentic answers. However, there are differences in some of the results.

TEAM OBSERVATION

This technique is most often used when research and marketing people want nothing between them and a direct, hands-on, face-to-face experience with the consumer. No one edits or interprets the consumer for them. They get to see and hear everything for themselves.

After recruiting a small number of respondents (eight to twenty), a team of research and marketing professionals, notebooks at the ready, enter each home and watch consumers use the product or service at issue. They might stand just outside the bathroom door at 6:00 A.M. and watch family members brush their teeth, or linger in the kitchen while the evening meal is prepared and then join the family around the dinner table. Or the visit could be spent at the computer center observing what software is being used and who's using it, or around the barbecue grill, or the basketball hoop attached to the garage. The team might accompany respondents to the beach, to a picnic site, on a shopping trip, or even to a restaurant. There are almost no restrictions on the areas of the home or external sites where observation might be performed.

FIGURE 3.1

The family gets ready for dinner.

When they get back to their offices or their hotel each day, team members meet to compare notes. What did they learn so far? Are they looking in the right places? Are they asking the right questions? Are there more fruitful areas of inquiry? Should any of the questions be dropped? Generally, the project continues for at least three or four days, giving team members an opportunity to hone the interviews and explore unexpected potentials that turn up along the way. Findings are written up at the end of the project, and recommendations for action are presented to management.

Advantages of Team Observation

Team observation can yield the following positive results:

- Researchers and marketing members of the team get to meet and understand their customers directly.

- The team is not at the mercy of interpreters with axes to grind, vested interests in particular approaches, or misunderstandings about the category.

- The people responsible for marketing and advertising strategy become more knowledgeable about consumer habits, practices, and attitudes concerning their product and product category than others in the company are.

- With the knowledge team members gain directly, it is often easier for them to exercise control over the marketing process.

Limitations of Team Observation

The following disadvantages characterize team observation:

- Team members must spend days on end away from the office and often out of town.

- The more people who observe consumers using a product, the more self-conscious consumers usually are. Actions and reactions may be far from natural when four or five people are hanging over a consumer's shoulder as she brushes her teeth or hovering around the family while they're eating dinner. Respondents are less likely to divulge highly personal revelations.

- A major advantage to the team may be a disadvantage to management. Those present at the interviews will interpret, organize, and present the findings from the interviews as they see fit and sometimes with a political agenda. There is often no record of specific actions and commentary other than the team's notes. Those paying for the study may have no opportunity to secure an objective point of view on the raw material. Management must rely purely on the judgment of team members.

STILL CAMERA AND AUDIOTAPE

This is the method favored by many academically trained anthropologists and ethnographers. Generally, one or two researchers are involved. They take a still camera and a hand-held audiotape recorder into a consumer's home. Researchers follow procedures similar to those described for the team, but with this method everything is on record. Scores of photos, sometimes as many as a hundred, are taken in the course of one interview. Everything significant to the product category, from medicine cabinet contents to the condition of the shower stall to the kinds of shoes in a man's closet, is photographed. All consumer comments and all responses to questions are captured on the audiotape recorder.

FIGURE 3.2

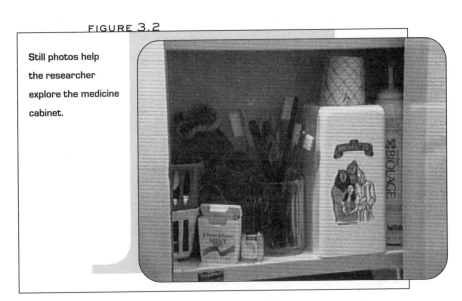

Still photos help the researcher explore the medicine cabinet.

Advantages of Still Camera and Audiotape

This technique offers significant advantages:

- With the interview on record, fewer people need to be present. It's easier for the researchers to create an open, easy relationship with members of the household. There's less chance that respondents will feel self-conscious. Their actions and reactions are likely to be more natural and their personal revelations more intimate.

- It's easier and less distracting when fewer people accompany a respondent on a shopping trip.

- When one or two people perform the interview instead of four or five, there's less chance for it to ramble. The flow is easier to perceive. The time spent with each consumer is often more efficiently used, and the results are clearer and more analyzable.

- The information generated by the research is easily manipulated and studied. Photographs documenting the interviews can be taped to a wall, placed in an album, or scanned into a computer and organized by respondents or subject matter and the related audiotape portion played against them. The interviews can be recapitulated and reorganized again until the issues become clear.

- The raw material of the interviews is accessible to all concerned parties. No one person or group owns the data. Management can more easily offer objective input and constructive criticism of the findings.

- Personnel time and travel expenses are kept to a minimum.

Limitations of Still Camera and Audiotape

This technique has several disadvantages:

- Body language and facial expressions are often more revealing than are a respondent's words. A researcher would have to be very lucky to catch any of this material with a still camera: the apprehensive way a child looks at a forkful of unfamiliar food before taking a bite; the expression of resignation that flickers across a woman's face as she prepares to do the laundry for the umpteenth time; a man's proprietary stance in front of his car.

- Presentations of interview excerpts to support findings can be somewhat tedious and awkward.

- Returning to the original data can be equally tedious.

VIDEOTAPE

This technique is often employed when the end use of the research is for both marketing and advertising purposes or for new product development. Usually an interviewer and a cameraperson with a compact professional videotape camera visit a consumer's home and record the entire interview—usage and storage of product, personal reactions, and lifestyle—on videotape. In the tradition of documentary films, the cameraperson becomes like a fly on the wall, reducing his or her presence to the point at which the respondent forgets that the camera is there. The interviewer engages and relaxes the consumer.

Sometimes a videotape camera may be set to run on site without the presence of either the cameraperson or the interviewer. For example, if the observational project consists of a day in the life of a computer—to see who in the family uses it, how much time people spend in front of the screen, and what Internet site is visited most often or what programs are most employed—the camera can be trained on the computer and left running. The same kind of exploration can be made in front of the family refrigerator.

Once in a while, it may be advantageous to ask a family member to videotape certain activities, particularly when it would be impossible or awkward for the researcher to be present. Kids playing together in a tree house, for example, could

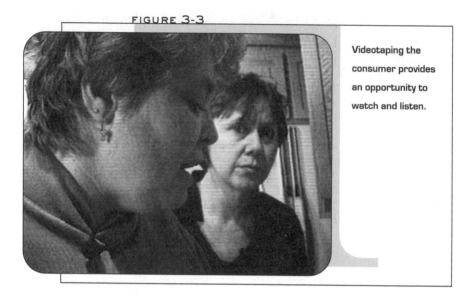

FIGURE 3-3

Videotaping the consumer provides an opportunity to watch and listen.

film themselves. The footage might be awful from a technical point of view, but it is real, and it's usually supplemented by professional, on-camera interviews in the homes.

For in-store observation and interviewing, hidden cameras may be trained on a particular aisle. When shoppers make an appropriate selection, they are approached and asked if they would mind being interviewed in front of an open camera for a small fee. Or recruited shoppers might be followed, videotaped, and interviewed throughout their entire shopping trip.

Advantages of Videotape

Videotape is often selected for these advantages:

- Videotape is the next best thing to being there. It allows all interested parties to see and hear everything that goes on in the interview.

- Nothing is lost: the way a consumer handles a bottle of cooking oil or applies a body lotion to his skin; the dynamics of family interaction in the kitchen as the pasta boils; the grin of satisfaction after a camera user gets that perfect picture; the crunch of a potato chip in a school cafeteria; the anger and frustration a computer user allows herself when a program doesn't work the way it's supposed to work. All verbal and body language and every action, reaction, and nuance are recorded forever on videotape.

- Videotaped interviews can be reviewed by supervisors at distant locations as they are completed, and directions to the interviewer can be amended for subsequent interviews.

- Findings and supportive material are easily organized on videotape.

- Videotape is a highly accessible form of qualitative research. The raw interviews are easily available for analysis by anyone involved in the project. The videotape summary can be duplicated endlessly for anyone with an interest in the research.

Limitations of Videotape

Videotape has its drawbacks:

- Once in a great while a respondent will freeze up in front of the video camera. In these rare instances, a respondent may have to be replaced.

- It's hard to get permission from a store or store chain to use a videotape camera in the aisles.

- Sometimes while videotaping a close-up of the hands in action, the cameraperson may miss a facial expression, and vice versa.

- Because it is so accessible, the summary tape's revelations are fair game for anyone in the organization to criticize, dispute, or deny.

- Some researchers feel the camera is more intrusive than an audiotape recorder.

COMBINED TECHNIQUE

Some companies have used a form of observational research that combines team observation, a still camera in the hands of the respondent, and follow-up focus groups involving storytelling and other projective methodologies. This technique is sometimes used to reveal the inner feelings of notoriously uncommunicative consumers—teenagers, for example.

The combined technique might begin with the team observing respondents in their everyday lives. Then researchers would give them 35mm still cameras and ask the respondents to photograph parts of their lives by themselves or with their friends—those parts relevant to the product category. Later, respondents might meet in a focus group and show the photographs they took to their friends. The moderator might ask other members of the focus group to make up stories about some of the photos the respondents took. During the process, strong feelings concerning the product category and the brands often come out.

The pictures, stories, and responses are analyzed. And on the basis of the feelings that have been revealed, new marketing concepts and new ways of communicating the brand to the consumer segment are developed.

Advantages of the Combined Technique

The combined technique offers these advantages:

- It offers a way for outsiders to find out what members of a noncommunicative group are really thinking and feeling about their lives, themselves, and the product involved.

- The methodology can turn up attitudes and insights that could offer advertisers a new way of reaching the potential consumer, one in which they are not ordinarily reached.

- With the exception of the process of taking photographs, the team can be involved in the whole process.

Limitations of the Combined Technique

The combined technique suffers from some limitations:

- The entire process may take eight or nine weeks—somewhat longer than other forms of observational research.

- The combined technique is dependent on the revelations provided by the photographs, which are often shot by respondents who may not know how to say something with a camera.

- Peer-group pressure may be a big factor in the follow-up focus group, distorting insights and conclusions.

AUTHOR'S RECOMMENDATION

There are reasons both practical and political to select any one of the techniques or any combination of them for your next observational research project. But experience shows that the combination of videotaping and depth interviewing offers not only the most intimate details of a consumer's everyday life with your product, but also the fullest, most complete depiction of the product experience. Also, in this age of not enough time and not enough people to do all the things a company needs to get done, a videotape summary may be the quickest, easiest way to gain an in-depth understanding of consumers.

DON'T TRY IT!

The worst technique you could possibly employ in observational research is that of having nonprofessionals from your company visit a home by themselves and watch the consumer use your product. Your people may be the most perceptive, insightful, and objective individuals imaginable, but two negative outcomes of such a visit can be guaranteed. First, they will bring with them a vested interest in the product and in the outcome of the interview. Without saying a word, they will communicate to the respondent the way they want the interview to go and the attitudes they hope will come out. And the respondent will respond accordingly. The result: a prejudiced insight and a prejudiced conclusion. If you go, always let an observational research professional ask the questions and do the probing. If there's something more that needs to be explored, go through the interviewer who cares only about doing a good job and getting at the truth and not about the success of your product.

WHAT THIS CHAPTER TELLS YOU

- Almost any observational technique provides detailed documentation of the product experience and how consumers relate to it.

- Team observation allows interested parties to see and hear consumers directly and maintain control, but it requires team members to be out of the office for extended periods.

- Still camera and audiotape observation is usually performed by two researchers who may be anthropologists. Consumer reactions are more natural when fewer people are observing, but body language and subtle expressions can be lost without a visual, in-motion record.

- Videotape takes in everything. Nothing is lost. Everything is accessible. But some people feel the video camera is too intrusive.

- The combined technique lets you customize your observational research to suit your special needs. But the process may take longer.

PLANNING THE OBSERVATIONAL RESEARCH PROJECT:

HOW TO MAKE SURE YOU GET

WHAT YOU WANT

Not long ago a research firm was asked to perform ethnography—specifically observational research—among consumers for a health food processor. When the researchers asked what the client wanted to find out, they were told that the company was excited about ethnography, that "They were interested in a general exploration, to see what this technique might turn up." Repeated requests for more specific objectives were turned aside. The company had never used this kind of research before, so the researchers were told, and they wanted to see if ethnography would provide insights other kinds of research hadn't come up with.

Against their better judgment, members of the research firm went ahead with the project. They videotaped consumers as they sought their nutritionists' advice. They recorded the advice given about the kind of health food to buy. Then they followed each consumer into a health food store or supermarket to watch them get additional advice from a salesperson before buying a product. They accompanied them home to videotape them preparing the food and eating it, and they interviewed respondents every step of the way.

The project was long and involved. And at the end, when the ninety-minute videotape summary was completed, the client had a predictable reaction: "We didn't learn anything we didn't know already."

The moral is that what you get from observational research depends on what you put into it. For all its potential to turn up insights and ideas unavailable from other forms of qualitative or quantitative research, observational research requires the answer to two simple questions before even one interview takes place: Who will benefit from the research, and what do they want to get out of the project?

Who will actually use the findings? Management? Market research people? R&D? Package designers? Your advertising agency? Sales promotion? Or all of the above? Each will have different questions it wants answered. Each will bring different expectations to the research. Knowing who will benefit will help you set up the objectives, ask the right questions, and ensure that the final presentation is developed for the right audience.

It should also be determined, as much as possible, how the observational research study will mesh with other studies the company may be planning. Will it guide a quantitative study? Will focus groups be conducted on the same issues? How will the observational findings be evaluated in the light of other research?

The Objective Imperative

Setting objectives is the single most important part of the planning. Without clear, well thought-out objectives, observational research—like any other form of research—is bound to disappoint.

That said, there are a wide variety of potential objectives observational research using ethnographic techniques can fulfill—often with unique results. And the results can be brought to life, not just depicted with graphs and bullet points. Here are only some of many possible objectives:

- To understand what the product or service means in the lives of its consumers

- To learn how consumers actually use a product in their everyday lives

- To uncover in-use motivations

- To reveal unmet needs

- To document the real benefits consumers experience as they use a product

- To understand the way consumers prepare and eat a food product or category

- To probe problems and opportunities associated with packaging

- To understand and document the quality of suffering and relief provided by medication

- To uncover consumer language, cues, and signals for potential use in advertising executions

- To learn selection and purchase behavior at the store

- To document response to in-store promotions and signage

- To learn how consumers plan their food shopping

- To generate new products

- To test new products

- To develop use-generated positioning and repositioning

- To uncover in-home decision points concerning product purchase and usage

- To understand the emotional relationship between consumers and their clothes

- To determine the product or category satisfactions and dissatisfactions

- To identify and understand a lifestyle

These are specific, marketing-oriented objectives, and observational research is well-suited to fulfill any one of them and others in addition. There are as many objectives as there are questions about how consumers purchase, use, and react to products in their everyday lives. Observational research can also be used for broader purposes, such as a study of a complete market segment, as indicated in the first chapter. Such projects can provide a surprising look at potentially profitable markets. The detailed findings frequently become primary source material for the company's research and development group and market research department.

RESIST ISSUE GREED!

How many objectives can one observational study fulfill? The fewer the objectives, the more in depth the results will be. Confining the project to two or three objectives allows researchers to document and probe each issue in detail. And it's the personal details that often provide the special insights and ideas available through ethnographic research.

But greedy marketers have a tendency to tack on extra issues. When you hear the phrase, "As long as they're going to be in the home . . . ," you know what's coming. "It's an interesting issue, why not cover it? And by the way, we have another product that we'd like to throw in as well, just to get a quick in-home consumer reaction." When this kind of thing happens, the result is always the same: research sprawl and superficial coverage of all the issues.

For the sake of a project and its outcome, it's important to resist the quadruple objectives and the add-ons that suggest a whole different purpose, and keep the goals to a minimum. A good test of objectives is to try writing them in one clear, uncomplicated sentence. If you can do that, you're on the way to a pointed, productive study.

THE PROPOSAL

The proposal is an outline of the project—the issues to be covered, who will be recruited, what's going to be observed, the kinds of questions the interviewer will ask, what form the findings will take, timing, and costs. Whether yours is the company performing the research or the one that hires the observational research firm, you should insist on a clear, detailed, well-conceived proposal and not just a timing and budget memorandum.

Here's an example of a proposal written for a manufacturer of plastic bags for trash and garbage disposal. (The brand and company name are not shown in order to protect proprietary information.)

This is a relatively broad-based proposal. When particular products are explored, the proposal may include issues as specific as the ways consumers make the ketchup come out of the bottle or the steps they follow when they connect a new computer or lay flooring tile.

OBJECTIVES

- To understand how consumers hold, sort, and dispose of their trash

- To uncover problems and frustrations involved in handling trash—particularly those not currently addressed by available products

- To help open potential areas for new trash-handling product development or current product repositioning

METHODOLOGY

- Housecalls will videotape and interview consumers in their homes in two or three separate suburban areas to discover where and how they store various kinds of trash, how they sort their trash, and how they dispose of it.

Detail

- There are various kinds of common household trash:
    —Garbage generally developed in the kitchen
    —Wastebasket trash (usually accumulated in bathrooms, bedrooms, home offices, etc.)
    —Newspapers and magazines
    —Dead leaves and grasses (probably seasonal)
    —Heavy-duty cleaning trash (possibly seasonal)

In addition, trash can be categorized as wet or dry, organic or nonorganic, cans, bottles, plastic, or metal.

Housecalls will seek to understand whether consumers in various parts of the country make these distinctions and whether they treat different kinds of trash in different ways.

- Half the recruitment will take place in areas with strong recycling mandates and half in areas with no strong recycling laws. Respondents will be told not to empty their garbage or wastebaskets before the interview.

- Housecalls will perform a visual inventory of all the trash in each household, encouraging respondents to talk about the origins and frequency of trash accumulation in each case. Respondents will be probed on the benefits and problems associated with each trash receptacle, covering the following issues:
    —General appropriateness for specific trash
    —Adequacy of size
    —Weight or thickness of material
    —Durability/breakage
    —Leakage
    —Sanitation
    —Closure

—Odor containment
—Aesthetic concerns
—Disposability
—Cost
—Other problem issues

- Respondents will then be asked to empty trash containers as they normally do: into larger bags, garbage cans, or whatever the final disposal container may be. If respondents usually sort trash in any way, they will be asked to do so at this point.

- The interviewer will probe respondents on these issues as they relate to final disposal containers.

- In addition, the interviewer will probe respondents concerning trash collection or disposal at the local dump. What are the local requirements concerning the receptacles respondents use? Does what they use meet these requirements adequately? If not, why not?

- Interviews will last approximately one hour.

- Taped interviews will be sent express mail each night to Housecalls for logging and analysis and further direction, if required. The client will be informed continuously as the assignment proceeds about significant attitudes and practices.

Deliverables for Client

- Housecalls will provide a summary of the findings. A transcript of the interview excerpts and videotape narration will be prepared. The summary tape will contain a detailed examination of habits, practices, and attitudes concerning trash disposal. The tape will note problem areas, product gaps, potential positioning opportunities for current products, and areas for new product development.

- Raw footage of all interviews will be available as well.

TIMING AND COSTS

- The initial setup (screener, interview guide) will be completed before the end of May. Housecalls fieldwork (recruitment, video-taping, and interviewing) will be completed about the third week in June 1996. The completed assignment will be delivered before the middle of July.

- The cost of study with thirty respondents (three different sub-urbs) is $00,000 +/− 10 percent, plus travel expenses for the interviewer and camerawoman and for Housecalls personnel to client headquarters, if deemed necessary.

- The cost of study with twenty-five respondents (two different suburbs) is $00,000 +/− 10 percent, plus travel expenses for the interviewer and camerawoman and for Housecalls personnel to client headquarters, if deemed necessary.

- One-half of the fee is due at the initiation of the project. One-half is due when the project is completed.

THE INTERVIEW GUIDE

The interview guide (some call it the *discussion guide*) is common to all forms of qualitative research. The interview guide is used in focus groups, mall intercepts, telephone interviews, and on the Internet. The interview guide has as its main purpose exactly what the name suggests: to take the interviewer and interviewee through the issues that need to be explored. It also has a second purpose: to detail for all interested parties the specific areas of inquiry and the general flow of the interview. It's the last opportunity to influence the research before the field-work begins, and frequently one or more people involved in the project add to it their pet questions. If the proposal is the project outline, then the interview guide is the blueprint for the project.

The interview guide differs somewhat from guides used for other kinds of qualitative research. Most other guides assume an interviewer or moderator will control the discussion, moving respondents along from topic A to topic B within a given time frame and making sure that all the issues are covered. In a focus group, for example, unproductive arguments among participants and forays into irrelevant side issues need to be monitored and the discussion brought back on track. In a mall intercept the questions are usually asked by the numbers, and the interviewer is expected to stick more or less to the order. However, when an observational researcher enters a consumer's home, the best thing that can happen is that the consumer rather than the interviewer becomes the dominant person in the interview. While the interviewer has to make sure that all the issues are covered, the most productive interviews take place when the interviewer gives over the lead and allows the respondent to take the interview into surprising, unanticipated areas. (More on this in a subsequent chapter.)

The observational research interview guide draws a fine line between a public document and a key to the private, intimate relationship that needs to be established between the interviewer and the respondent. It allows those paying for the research to visualize the interview in complete detail—the actions to be observed, the questions to be asked, the topics to be covered. At the same time, it must encourage a relaxed, free-wheeling exchange between the respondent and the interviewer—in which both are open to anything that comes up. The guide should allow for the order and even the emphasis to change, depending upon what the respondent does or says during the course of the interview. And it must allow the interviewer to conduct the interview in his or her own style, using his or her own words.

> **The observational interview should be a voyage of discovery, and the guide must reflect and anticipate the possibility of venturing into uncharted waters.**

Here's an example of a guide developed for an in-home study on videotape of athlete's foot sufferers. In-home observation was used for this study because respondents sometimes find it difficult to talk in depth about their condition in front of strangers in a focus group. It was felt that sufferers would be more revealing in their homes, in front of an accepting interviewer. Respondents were recruited in the initial stages of athlete's foot. There were two objectives:

1. To gain insight into the athlete's foot experience:

   - The physical and emotional quality of their discomfort

   - The sense of relief afforded by the medication they use

   - The expectation and reality of their cure

2. To uncover visual and verbal cues and signals for potential use in advertising executions

This guide contains all the issues to be explored, but its telegraphic headings allow the interviewer to use his or her own words in asking each question. And in actual practice, this interviewer was encouraged to spend more time on the topics that interested respondents the most. One sufferer, a mail carrier being interviewed in his home, took up a lot of the interview with vivid expressions of the burning and itching he was experiencing at the moment. With other respondents, the interviewer concentrated more on the sights and sounds of relief, uncovering a variety of ways sufferers experienced their medication as it calmed the pain.

INTERVIEW GUIDE: ATHLETE'S FOOT SUFFERERS

While the cameraperson sets up, the interviewer dispenses the check, gets the release signed, explains Housecalls methodology and purpose of research (companies need to gain knowledge in order to make better remedies), and puts the respondent at ease.

I. THE CONDITION

A. *Background*

- How often have athlete's foot?

- Last time?

- Suffering how long this time? *Ascertain first three or four days.*

- How and where picked up?

- Anything done to prevent getting condition? What?

- Condition considered chronic?

  At this point, the interviewer asks the respondent to show the camera the condition.

B. *Symptoms*

- How describe the way it looks?

- How describe the way it feels? *Encourage the respondent to verbalize specific words and sounds used—curses included.*

- Special smell?

- Reaction when first noticed symptoms? *Encourage additional verbalization.*

- How it feels during the day (on the job, walking around, etc.)?

2. SOCIAL EFFECTS

- Affect mood now or during the day? How? *Ascertain if the current mood is normal or modified by the condition.*

- Affect relationship with others? How? *Probe how intimacy is affected.*

- Affect job? How?

- Think of self as different, alienated from others with condition?

- Think of self as less able? How?

- Prevent normal activities? Which? Why?

- Think of condition as contagious?

- Afraid of giving condition to others?

- Ways of preventing spreading condition to others?
    —At home (shower, sheets, floor, etc.)
    —In public places such as health club

3. RELIEF

A. Habits and Practices

- What remedy used? *Show. Camera notes where kept.*

- How many times a day used?

- How many days remedy used?

- Why that number of days?

- Usually, when and where?

- Used on regular schedule or in response to discomfort?

■ Take along away from home?

■ Generally, how feel about using?

    —Look forward?

    —Avoid?

    —Neutral?

    —Other (i.e., messy, oily, inconvenient)?

B. Relief Expected

■ Describe

■ Complete or partial?

■ All symptoms?

■ How long will relief last?

■ Relief same as cure? If different, how?

At this point, the interviewer asks the respondent to use his or her remedy in front of the camera. The camera notes the amount of remedy applied and the method of application and then goes immediately to the face to note the potential expression of relief.

C. Relief Achieved

■ Describe immediate sensation of relief. Encourage respondent to verbalize words and sounds as symptoms abate.

■ Describe relief as it continues to take effect.

■ Usual method/amount of application?

■ More medication better/worse? Why?

■ Feel any different in general? *Note change of mood, if any.*

■ How feet feel after medication has taken effect?

D. Other Forms of Relief

- What do during day to feel relief?

- Loosen/take off shoes?

- Reapply medicine?

- Apply additional substances? What?

- Other?

4. The Medication

- Why that form? (spray or shake powder, ointment)

- Positives/negatives about form

- Why that brand?

- Positives/negatives about brand

- Expect complete/partial cure?

- How long before cure?

- Time reasonable/unreasonable?

- How could be better?

- Ideal athlete's foot medication (wish list)?

- Ever use to *prevent* athlete's foot?

- Where normally keep? *Note if the medication is hidden away, kept out, or kept with other* OTC *products. Probe for a potential sense of embarrassment or other feelings about using the medication.*

5. Epilogue

The interviewer asks the respondent to put on shoes and socks. The camera notes if care is taken to prevent the spread of the condition or medication.

The interviews produced a number of unanticipated insights. One was the discovery that athlete's foot often deprives some sufferers of sleep. The itching and the burning actually wakes them up. Another important insight was that, for some respondents, there was a deep sense of shame associated with athlete's foot, a feeling of uncleanness.

In a perfect research world, every interview would cover every issue in the guide. In actual practice, some interviews emphasize one thing and others something else. For instance, if you're involved with a food product, a good part of the interview might concern the package—how difficult it is to open, how the respondent can't read the directions, how respondents wish it would be smaller so it could fit more easily in their freezers or pantries, and how they can't seem to find it in the stores very easily.

This is great information, but what about the way the consumer you're visiting prepares the product? That part of the interview might have to get short shrift. Go where the respondent goes and wait for the next consumer to show and tell you more about preparation. Here is one obvious conclusion: Make sure you have enough respondents to explore the major issues. It is unwise to recruit fewer than fifteen.

The key to planning an observational research project is maintaining an adroit balance between a carefull choreography and a loosey-goosey willingness to let the interview go where it will. After all the thinking and the planning, the relationship established between the interviewer and the respondent will determine much of how and where the interview goes.

How are the respondents selected for observational research projects? You'll find out in the next chapter. Whether you're in management or research, it will serve you well to make sure the consumers that are studied fit the marketing profile of your brand.

WHAT THIS CHAPTER TELLS YOU

- Be clear, simple, and single-minded when you develop your objectives.

- Insist on a well-conceived proposal. The proposal is the seed. Everything—including the final results—grows out of it.

- A good interview guide ensures that the interviewer addresses all the relevant issues, but it is not rigid. It should allow the interviewer to launch a voyage of discovery, come what may.

- The most productive observational research interviews follow the lead of the respondent.

5

RECRUITMENT:

HOW TO MAKE SURE THE RIGHT
CONSUMERS ARE OBSERVED

This is an age in which people hang up on researchers conducting a survey and wave off research recruiters in the mall.
So how do you find people willing to allow observational
researchers into their homes to watch them sometimes performing intimate personal business? And how do you make sure they're
the right people?

You'll discover that almost 80 percent of the people who are
asked are willing. One big incentive is money. Respondents are
offered an incentive that can vary from sixty to two hundred dollars for an interview of a couple of hours' duration, depending on
the product or service category, the complexity of the interview,
and the action required of the respondent. An interview that asks
a consumer to make a meal and then serve it to his or her family,
for example, will call for a larger incentive than will a study of a
consumer vacuuming a rug. A project that watches respondents
taking a shower (yes, that's been done) will need a hefty incentive.
Recruitment of kids drinking soda is relatively cheap.

But, beyond money, people today snatch the opportunity to be
heard, to show and tell the powers controlling the commercial
parts of their lives who they are, what they like, what they don't
like, and the improvements they want in the products and services

they need. Unlike a survey, observational research is a highly personal forum for respondents, complete with live demonstration. It's also a way for them to take back some control of a part of their lives—to act upon the marketing complex instead of being acted upon.

And many people are genuinely curious about the procedure. When the request comes from a legitimate source, most people go along with the project just to see what it's all about.

HELP WITH RECRUITMENT

As any researcher can tell you, the worst way to recruit is to try to do it through your own company—that is, unless you're a professional recruiter. Professional recruitment is just the help you need.

Throughout the United States, in almost any area in which you'd want to perform an observational project, there are companies specializing in recruitment for qualitative research. They have databases of thousands of people in every age group, at every income and education level, and in practically every product or service category. You want sixty-year-old users of denture adhesive? Professional recruiters will find them for you. Looking for women loyal to Mazola Cooking Oil? Owners of Harley Davidsons? Affluent tennis players? Two-computer families? They've got them on file.

These companies are listed in the yellow pages of the American Marketing Association's *GreenBook* under "Focus Group: Recruitment" or "Field Service," which is what they're commonly called. And you'll also find them in the AMA's *Focus Group Directory*. Most of these companies now have experience recruiting for observational research. If you are planning an observational research project abroad, you might want to check in the annual *Directory of International Marketing Research Firms*, published in *Marketing News*.

It is impossible to give a definitive cost of using a recruitment company. Prices change from region to region, and they change with the times. Suffice it to say that recruitment costs represent a relatively small percentage of the total cost of a project.

DEVELOPING THE RECRUITMENT SPECIFICATIONS

With one or two exceptions, the specifications for observational recruitment (like the screener we'll cover shortly) are pretty much the same as those for other forms of qualitative research, such as focus groups. So, if you're familiar with qualitative specs and screeners, skip the samples printed here. If not, the models that follow will help you know what to expect when you're involved with observational research.

After the objectives, the second most important document you need for an observational research project is less than one page long. It's called the *spec sheet*, and it tells your recruiter and everyone else involved what kinds of consumers you expect to interview.

> The kinds of consumers you interview have everything to do with the kinds of results you get.

Start your thinking about recruitment with the research objectives. For example, if the purpose of your study is to find out why consumers don't consume more of your product, you may want to recruit beyond your standard regular user. Light users or consumers who use a competitive product might tell you worlds about your product's problems.

If the objective is to find opportunities for new products within a category, you'll probably need a wide spectrum of current users of various brands. Want some fresh consumer language for advertising executions? Be sure to recruit people capable of expressing themselves. The absolute minimum in terms of demographics for the spec sheet are age, income, gender, education, family status, place of residence, and current product usage.

Psychographics and Lifestyle

Beyond these basic qualifications, you might want to add *psychographics*, the attitudes people have about themselves, their lives, and their futures. Psychographic specifications tell you, for example, whether consumers think and act as if they're just about making it in life or if, on the other hand, they think of themselves as having an unlimited future. The difference in that one attitude could be the deciding factor in a big-ticket purchase, such as a car. It could also be the reason a consumer allows himself or herself to purchase an imported premium beer.

SRI, a well-known research firm, has developed a system called VALS ™ to determine consumer psychographics. Here is an outline of SRI's various attitudinal categories:

VALS Segment Descriptions (Abridged)

Actualizers: Actualizers are successful, sophisticated, active, "take-charge" people with high self-esteem and abundant resources. They're interested in growth and self-expression. They have a wide range of interests and are open to change. Their tastes are highly cultivated.

Fulfilleds: Fulfilleds are mature, satisfied, comfortable people who value order, knowledge, and responsibility. Most are well educated, well informed, and interested in broadening their knowledge. They are often conservative, practical, and family centered. They look for durability, functionality, and value in the products they buy.

Achievers: Achievers are successful career- and work-oriented people who feel in control of their lives. They value stability and predictability over risk and self-discovery. Their lives are structured around career, family, and church. They live conventional lives and favor prestige products that demonstrate success to their peers.

Experiencers: Experiencers are young, vital, enthusiastic, impulsive, and rebellious. They seek variety and excitement, savoring the new, the offbeat, and the risky. They quickly become interested in new possibilities but are equally quick to cool. They have an abstract disdain for conformity but are in awe of others' wealth and power. They're avid consumers who spend much of their income on clothing, fast food, music, movies, and videos.

Believers: Believers are conservative, conventional, and traditional. Many live by an expressed moral code. Their lives follow established routines, mostly organized around the home, family, and social or religious organizations. They favor American products and established brands. Their income and education are modest but sufficient to meet their needs.

Strivers: Strivers seek motivation, self-definition, and approval from others. They are unsure of themselves, and low on economic, social, and psychological resources. Strivers are impulsive and easily bored. Many seek to be stylish, attempting to emulate those who own the possessions they covet but that are beyond their means.

Makers: Makers are practical people who have constructive skills and value self-sufficiency. They have few interests outside the context of family, practical work, and physical recreation. Most experience the world by working on it—building a house, raising children, fixing a car, or canning vegetables. They are suspicious of new ideas and respectful of government except when it intrudes on individual rights. Makers are unimpressed by material possessions, except those that are practical, such as tools.

Strugglers: Strugglers live constricted lives. They're chronically poor, poorly educated, unskilled, and often resigned. Their chief concerns are security and safety. Strugglers are cautious consumers. They represent a very modest market for most products and services but are loyal to favorite brands.

You may need an entirely different scale of psychographics for your project, depending upon the product or service category at issue. For example, the degree to which emotion or reason governs respondents' decisions or the quotient of optimism versus pessimism concerning the future could make all the difference in a consumer's decision to make a major purchase. Whatever scale you use (if you do decide to recruit on the basis of psychographics), a brief description of the psychographic segment you want would be helpful to the recruiter.

Lifestyle can be part of or separate from psychographics. If you're dealing with a product or service that expresses personal identity—the way a consumer wants to appear to the world—you'll probably need to describe the kind of lifestyle you're looking for. Lifestyle may or may not relate to income. Lifestyle is the *way* a person spends his or her money, not necessarily the amount of money spent.

Do consumers spend most of their time and energy making their home beautiful? Or do they put a lot of their money into travel? Or does your audience consist of young people who spend most of their money on clothes? And what's their level of taste? Upscale? Sophisticated? Or middlebrow? If your product is a Tourneau watch, you'll want a fashion-conscious respondent with upscale tastes. Gap jeans might call for a completely different type of respondent. (Although don't be surprised if you find your respondent wearing both Gap jeans and a Tourneau watch.)

Consider special interests when the product category calls for it: sports or fitness, parenting, retirement, and corporate life. Don't forget people who like a certain kind of music or who are gay. You may want even finer distinctions.

And, finally, decide how many respondents are necessary for the study. With fewer than fifteen, there will be a good chance that a few oddballs will give you the wrong idea about product usage or about the benefits most consumers see in the product. With more than fifty, the results take longer to get. And they're more difficult to analyze in depth. In addition, a larger study starts to build quantitative expectations as in, "Over half the people said the taste sucks, so that's the way everyone's going to think." Remember: observational research is a qualitative tool. It's meant to generate direct, in-depth insights into the consumer experience. It's not a survey of the market.

Here's a typical spec sheet. It was developed for the athlete's foot study referred to earlier.

Condition: Must be suffering from athlete's foot, and must have started to experience the symptoms a maximum of three days ago

Age: 25–55 (We need a good spread.)

Gender: 16 men, 4 women

Income: $25,000–$100,000 household income per year (We need a spread, but emphasis should be on the lower income groups.)

Medication: Must use one of the major brands: Tinactin, Desenex, or Lotrimin. Some should use a shake powder, some a spray powder, and some a cream or ointment.

Education: All levels except grade school

Interview site: Home—whenever they use their medication (morning or evening)

In this case, psychographic and lifestyle qualifications were considered beside the point. Athlete's foot cuts across all attitudes and values. If you were doing a study of potential purchasers or leasers of luxury cars, your specifications might include the following:

Attitude: Must value an automobile as one of his or her most important possessions

Other possessions: Should own other luxury shelter or clothing possessions

THE SCREENER

How do recruiters actually go about recruiting? How do they screen out the people you don't want from the people you do? The observational or ethnographic screening process is little different from that performed for any other qualitative research. Recruiters will phone people they have listed on a large database, categorized demographically. Or in rare instances they'll phone consumers from a certain neighborhood at random. They'll ask some carefully conceived questions to determine the potential respondents' qualifications for the research, offer an incentive for their participation, and make appointments for the researchers to visit with them.

A good recruiter will rarely go back to the same people. And you should so specify in your screener. The last thing you want in any kind of qualitative research is a professional respondent.

Here's a screener prepared for an observational study of a new product prototype consisting of noodles and a flavored coating for chicken. (The brand and company name are disguised.) Notice how it begins with the widest universe and gradually winnows out potential respondents question by question, until it arrives at consumers who would be most receptive to the product category. Also note that the incentive offered potential respondents is seventy-five dollars, enough to allow an interviewer and a cameraperson into the respondent's home for an hour or so. Sometimes the incentive is greater, depending upon how involved the interview is going to be and how much of the respondent's time will be taken.

Brand Name Screener

Hello. My name is _____ from _____,
a research company in _____. We're conducting a
study on meals and would like to include your opinion. Do you
have time to answer a few questions?

1a. **Do you or anyone in your household work for:**

☐ a market research company or advertising agency?
(TERMINATE)

☐ a food processor, retailer, or wholesaler or any related
business? (TERMINATE)

☐ none of the above. (CONTINUE)

1b. **Have you participated in a market research study, focus
group, or telephone survey concerning any food product
during the last six months?**

☐ Yes. (TERMINATE)

☐ No. (CONTINUE)

2. **Do you shop and prepare meals for your family?**

☐ No. (TERMINATE)

☐ Yes. (CONTINUE)

3. **Does your family include at least one child between the
ages of:**

☐ 6 and 10? (CONTINUE)

☐ 10 and 13? (CONTINUE)

☐ 13 and 16? (CONTINUE)

☐ None of the above. (TERMINATE)

4. Is your spouse living with you at present?

☐ Yes.

☐ No.

At least fifteen families must include both husband and wife.

5. What category best describes your total annual household income?

☐ Under $30,000. (TERMINATE)

☐ $30,000–$40,000. (CONTINUE)

☐ $40,000–$50,000. (CONTINUE)

☐ $50,000–$60,000. (CONTINUE)

☐ Over $60,000. (CONTINUE)

Respondents' incomes should represent a spread.

6a. Do you sometimes prepare meals with one or more of the following side dishes?

☐ Prepackaged, flavored rice? (CONTINUE)

☐ Prepackaged, flavored, dried noodles? (CONTINUE)

☐ Prepackaged, flavored, dried pasta? (CONTINUE)

☐ None of the above. (TERMINATE)

6b. How frequently do you use these kinds of side dishes?

☐ Less than twice a month. (TERMINATE)

☐ At least twice a month. (CONTINUE)

7. I'm going to read the names of various brands to you. Please tell me if you've ever used them, if you've used them in the past three months, or if you've used them in the past month:

	Ever	Past three months	Past month
Kraft Rice & Cheese	☐	☐	☐
Noodle Roni	☐	☐	☐
Uncle Ben's Long Grain & Wild Rice	☐	☐	☐
Rice-A-Roni	☐	☐	☐
Savory Classics	☐	☐	☐
Uncle Ben's Country Inn	☐	☐	☐
Kraft Pasta & Cheese	☐	☐	☐
Golden Saute	☐	☐	☐
Lipton Rice & Sauce	☐	☐	☐
Lipton Noodles & Sauce	☐	☐	☐
Lipton Pasta & Sauce	☐	☐	☐

If respondent has not used any one of the above brands during the past month, TERMINATE.

If respondent has used at least one brand during the past month, CONTINUE.

8a. Have you used Hamburger Helper at any time during the past six months?

☐ No.

☐ Yes.

Respondents must include at least five Hamburger Helper users.

8b. Have you used Shake 'N Bake at any time during the past six months?

☐ No.

☐ Yes.

Respondents must include at least five Shake 'N Bake users.

9. How frequently do you serve your family chicken?

□ Less than once a week. (TERMINATE)

□ Once a week or more. (CONTINUE)

10a. Have you served pasta or noodles with an Alfredo flavor sometime in the past six months?

□ No.

□ Yes.

10b. Would you consider serving pasta or noodles with an Alfredo flavor?

□ No.

□ Yes.

If answer is no to questions 10a and 10b, TERMINATE.
If one answer is yes, CONTINUE.

A well-known food company would like to invite you to participate in a very unusual market research study. It would involve an interview in your home as you prepare and serve a meal to your immediate family. The interview would be conducted by two women and would last an hour to an hour and a half. The interview would be videotaped—but only for market research purposes. Your privacy would be completely respected. You would receive seventy-five dollars for your time and your participation, plus the cost of main ingredients other than those we would supply.

Respondent's name: _____

Address: _____

City: _____ State: _____ ZIP: _____

Home phone: _____ Office phone: _____

With a few questions—all easily and quickly answered—people not wanted for this particular study are weeded out, and precisely the people needed are secured for the research. Most qualitative research screeners follow this kind of format, sometimes with greater complexity—adding lifestyle or psychographic questions to home in on attitude, such as the following.

Which of these statements best describes the basic feeling you have about your future?

- I look forward to the future. Every year gets better.

- In general, I think the future will bring me good things. But it pays to be a little cautious about it.

- I think the future is uncertain. I try not to build up my hopes too much.

- I think things in the future are going to get worse rather than better.

Once recruiters start phoning, assuming thirty respondents or less, and the product or product category enjoys a reasonable incidence of usage, it should take no longer than seven business days for the recruitment firm to screen consumers, set a schedule, and provide whoever does the interviewing with clear directions. Obviously, under emergency conditions, respondents can be recruited much faster. But, if product users are difficult to find, allow at least seven days.

Recruiters will confirm your respondents the day before your appointment. If there's a cancellation or a no-show, they will scramble to provide an appropriate substitute.

It should be said, even if it's already apparent, that good recruiters are worth every penny you pay them. Their instincts for finding respondents with the most impossible specifications are sometimes downright astounding. I still don't know how our recruiter was able to find athlete's foot sufferers in precisely the second or third day of outbreak.

What This Chapter Tells You

- You should never do the recruiting yourself.

- There are several key resources to help you find a professional recruiter.

- You should never recruit fewer than fifteen consumers.

- Two simple documents can lead you to the right respondents—and the right findings.

- Think beyond demographics. Psychographics and lifestyle can tell you if your consumer is ready to buy—or resistant.

6

ON THE CONSUMER'S TURF:

INTERVIEWING AND DOCUMENTING THE PRODUCT EXPERIENCE

This chapter is about the guts of the observational research project—the actual process of observation while consumers use a product in their everyday environment. Whether your involvement with the nuts and bolts of the research process is minimal or you decide to tag along with the researcher, you should be aware of what actually happens when a good, experienced observer visits consumers on their home ground and of the possibilities for exploration and learning. You'll find that observing involves far more than passively watching.

THE INTERVIEWER AT WORK

How observational researchers handle themselves in a consumer's home, car, or office can mean the difference between a surprising, deeply revealing interview and a pat, routine interview with expected results. In general, there are two kinds of observational interviewers. The first kind is quiet, laid-back, unobtrusive, a good observer and listener, actively interested in everything the respondent does or says but careful not to impose. This person is adept at hanging out. The last thing you want is a researcher (or marketing person) who wants to take control and direct the interview. Even if nothing is communicated overtly, the attitudes the researcher or team member brings to the consumer will come across to the consumer, and the consumer will react accordingly.

The other kind of observational interviewer or researcher actively engages the respondent. There's a constant interaction between interviewer and respondent. Without taking control, the interviewer reacts to everything respondents do or say, at the same time gently prodding them to extend a discussion or do something they may be a little hesitant to do. This kind of interviewer is an active encourager.

Both kinds of respondents must remain totally nonjudgmental, no matter what the respondent does or says, no matter what condition the respondent's home is in.

It's a good idea to keep the same interviewer interviewing throughout the whole project. There is a cumulative learning process that takes place from interview to interview that works very much to the advantage of the project. The interviewer may discover in the course of the first five interviews, for example, that the product in question is not easily stored in many of the respondents' cabinets. He or she will be sure to probe the storage issue—even if it doesn't come up—in subsequent interviews.

It's also a good idea for the leader of the project or the analyst to be in daily touch with the interviewer, if only to act as an objective sounding board. Sometimes the person on the other end of the phone from the interviewer can help cut a line of questioning that isn't working, or to suggest a whole new area of observation.

If equipment is taken to the interview—a still or video camera or an audiotape recorder—it should be as compact as possible. No attempt should be made to hide a camera or tape recorder when the research team is in a consumer's home. The person handling the equipment should be up front about showing it to the respondents, so that they can quickly get used to its presence. You'll find the respondent begins not only to accept, but also to ignore the equipment before the first ten minutes of the interview have passed.

The ideal director of the interview—of its flow, its emphasis, and the forays into uncharted territory—is the respondent. The interviewer might have to make sure all the issues are covered, but how the respondent gets there should be up to the respondent.

As pointed out earlier, in-home observation has a great advantage over other forms of qualitative research in that it takes place on the respondent's own turf, in a familiar, comfortable environment. The consumer's words and actions are likely to be more natural, unconstrained by the unfamiliar surroundings of a facility and uncontaminated by the presence of strangers trying to show each other and the moderator how smart they are. A good observational interview is a conversation between people who are getting to know each other over the kitchen table or in front of a washing machine. It's easy, informal. Depending on the product category, it can be fun.

THE ART OF SILENCE

Most of the talk and all of the actions should come from the respondent. The interviewer and whoever else is present should play a secondary role. The questions should be brief. Think of them as triggers designed to start the flow of actions and words. The interviewer should not feel the need to jump in every time there's a pause in the conversation. When the impulse to fill those gaps is left to the respondent, what follows can lead to highly interesting revelations. Some interviewers have cultivated the encouraging "Uh huh" to a fine art. Examples abound of the value of just letting the respondent talk or do:

- The interviewer lets a dour woman suffering from heartburn read the paper while she waits for her medicine to take effect. After eight minutes of silence, a radiant smile of relief breaks across her face.

- A man in the throes of athlete's foot talks on and on about his condition without a word from the interviewer and finally despairs of ever being completely cured. "It's just part of life," he concludes.

- A student showing his collection of brand name sport clothes—one by one—ultimately reveals his desire for a reputation as someone who knows how to dress.

- An owner of a sick cat, totally ignoring the presence of the interviewer and accompanying cameraperson, explodes with financial anxiety when her vet suggests expensive testing.

A new subject is introduced only when the interviewer is sure the respondent has nothing more to add. And this points up another advantage of interviewing a person at home rather than among others in a focus group: At home, nobody else is waiting to get a word in. A topic can be exhausted. As respondents keep talking, they often articulate things they never knew they felt about the product experience. Sometimes they find themselves at a very revealing loss for words:

- When a baking soda–based underarm deodorant was first introduced to the market, an observational study was made of potential respondents. Many included women who were using baking soda as a deodorant for their refrigerators, but it often took the respondents five or ten minutes to make the connection between odor protection for food and odor protection under the arms. Their uncomprehending facial expressions made the manufacturer aware that it could not assume consumers would instantly see the value of a baking soda underarm deodorant. The personal deodorizing power of baking soda had to be played up both on the package and in the advertising.

- Trying to describe a new prototype flavor of a particular beverage, otherwise highly articulate respondents could only use nondescriptive words like "Good" or "Pleasant." The responses convinced R&D to go back to the drawing board and make the flavor more definitive.

- A woman looking for a particular toothbrush on a drugstore shelf was seen to clutch her fists in frustration before she walked away without finding what she wanted. This prompted a whole new look at the toothbrush shelf organization.

FIGURE 6.1

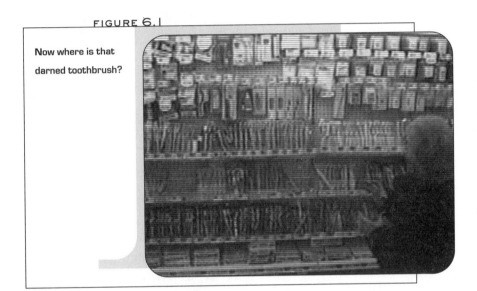

Now where is that darned toothbrush?

PROJECTIVE TECHNIQUES

Should the interviewer use the kinds of projective techniques employed in other forms of qualitative research? Questions like, "If this product were a movie star, who would it be?" work as well or as poorly in observational research. They are most effective in discussions about image or status-related products. But be careful when you ask projective questions in observational research. They tend to intrude upon the intimate ambiance and mood that should characterize the observational interview. With these questions the respondent is no longer showing and telling what he or she ordinarily does and thinks. Now the respondent is on the spot, and the interviewer has created—no matter how gently—the atmosphere of an exam. That will almost certainly affect the rest of the interview. If projective techniques are going to be used, they should be saved for the last few minutes.

At the end of the interview, the researcher should give the respondent the opportunity to have the last word. The last word may be the most telling because sometimes the things a respondent might have been hesitant to say come out at the end, when the interviewer encourages the respondent to say anything he or she has been dying to say. Now that they've spent all that time together, the embarrassing admission or the offbeat product usage is likely to come out more easily.

Others at the Interview

There will be times when a company feels strongly that a few of its personnel should be present in the consumer's home, along with the interviewer. This is all well and good. However, company people should stoutly resist the impulse to act as second, third, and fourth interviewers. If they engage the respondent in any kind of dialogue during the interview, it pollutes the intimate, one-on-one atmosphere the interviewer has worked so hard to build. If they do have questions, they'll have their chance to ask them after the interviewer has completely finished his or her probing.

Documenting Background and Lifestyle

Anything related to the product under consideration should be studied and recorded at the interview. How and where a product is stored can tell a lot about its place in the family's life. Is it in the back of the pantry or refrigerator, behind a competing food or beverage? Or is it out on the counter, ready to be used? What about the other food products on hand? What do they say about the importance of food to these people? The time they give to each meal? Their health concerns? Their taste preferences?

- An examination of a series of kitchen cabinets showed a flavored heat-and-serve noodle processor that its competition wasn't just other precooked noodles or pasta. The product was kept among other heat-and-serve starches the respondents had on hand: prepared potatoes and rice as well as precooked and uncooked noodles and pasta.

- A toy manufacturer discovered that in many homes with preteenagers, traditional board games were often stacked at the tops of closets, not easily reached by the kids they were meant for. The research brought them face-to-face with a strategic decision: They either had to make their games smaller and more accessible or put more emphasis on electronic games.

FIGURE 6.2

She's down there, and the board games are up here.

Wouldn't a music company, a computer or software maker, a sports equipment company, or a clothing manufacturer also like to know the contents of a preteen's room? How are his or her things organized? What's in the back of the closet? What's up front? What's just lying on the floor, and what's put away neatly?

Here's a storage-related example of a different kind: When a company developing a line of personal care products for seniors sent observers into the homes of intended customers, the researchers found that a big problem was storage space. Retired seniors and empty nesters often live in smaller homes than the homes they lived in with their families, so they have less room for the larger sizes of mouthwash, toothpaste, skin lotion, and other products in the money-saving economy size.

FIGURE 6.3

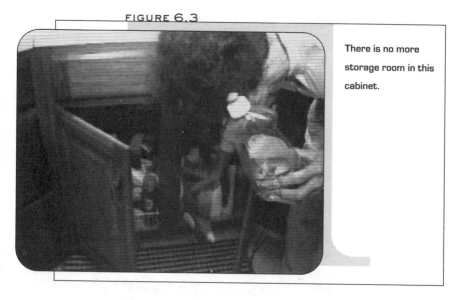

There is no more storage room in this cabinet.

If you're concerned with a health-care or personal care product, make sure to examine the contents of the family medicine chest. It will not only show what there's room for; it will also tell you what minor and not so minor physical problems people suffer from. The toothpaste formula, analgesic, soap, skin lotion, and shampoo will also show you how open family members are to new products and product advances. If they're using Bayer Aspirin, Ivory Soap, Jergen's Skin Lotion, and Head & Shoulders Shampoo, you can count on their brand loyalty, but you may find it hard to sell them a fancy new toothpaste technology.

Are there any brands deep within the pantry or medicine chest that look like they're from the year one? Why aren't they being used? What's replacing them? What made the users switch?

Consider clothing. Your product may be far removed from clothing. It may be something as distant as a cell phone or even a can of peas. But if what you sell has anything to do with the way consumers think about themselves, a few minutes in the closet during the interview will tell you reams about how to fit your product into their lives.

A researcher could have a field day documenting the contents of a working woman's clothes closet, discovering what she wears to the office and what she wears nights and weekends. Is she a different person when she goes to the office than when she goes out for fun or than when she hangs out at home? That's only one of the things her closet will tell you.

Not long ago, an interesting observational study for a brassiere company was conducted among large-breasted women. The assumption had been that women who needed a larger brassiere were primarily interested in support and comfort. The undergarments the company had been making for them were off-white and fairly plain. But when the research company examined respondents' clothing drawers, they found brassieres and panties of every color and design —from lacy, flower-covered Victoria's Secret styles to low-cut, brilliant red brassieres. Big-breasted women, it turned out, wanted to feel feminine and sexy too.

Look at the labels. They often represent—much as we may want to deny it—how people think of themselves and even how they value themselves. There are differences between the woman who buys from The Gap and the woman who buys from Banana Republic. And the differences may not have anything to do with age or income. We have found Armani and Polo labels in the closets of women whose family incomes are less than forty thousand dollars per year.

The same goes for men these days. In a world in which sportswear is more and more the standard everyday apparel, even at work, men's self-image and the way they differentiate themselves are expressed in new ways. Their clothes closets will reflect their personal identities.

Is there a home office? What electronic or mechanical equipment is involved? Where and how is it placed? Which supplies are immediately accessible? Which supplies are not? Who uses the equipment and when? Who doesn't use it and why? These same questions apply to almost any office in any large corporation.

The importance of this kind of background documentation can't be stressed enough. It's possible to examine the contents of a refrigerator, pantry, medicine chest, and clothes closet and extrapolate a family's entire lifestyle.

FOLLOWING CUES

An observational study, unlike most other forms of qualitative research, offers the researcher an opportunity to follow up on casual mentions and unarticulated actions—often leading to unforeseen insights and ideas such as the following:

- A manufacturer of single-use cameras had a research firm visit a popular zoo and hand out single-use cameras to people who hadn't used this particular compact, pocket-sized model before. Watching respondents take pictures of their families, researchers observed that they moved their fingers all around the camera, sometimes obscuring the lens, before they found the shutter button. In addition, many respondents with larger hands were unsure about how and where to grip the camera. Their fingers seemed to overwhelm the equipment.

A brief interview with each respondent after the pictures had been taken confirmed the observation. They didn't see where the shutter was at first. A pervasive concern was that, with such a small camera, their fingers might get in the way of the lens.

Clearly, the pocket-sized model needed to be more user friendly. The result was a redesign of the camera, making the model a little less compact (but still pocket sized) and the shutter more obviously accessible.

- Women applying a hand and body lotion in another observational study were seen to diverge into two kinds of users. Some slapped on the lotion, rubbing it briskly into their skin. Others caressed their skin as they applied it. Researchers found the difference interesting. After some probing, they discovered that the women who slapped it on used the lotion either as an antidote to or a restorative for dry skin. The women who applied the lotion slowly, on the other hand, were more interested in imparting something to their skin—softness or moisture. They enjoyed the experience, using it to relax for a few moments.

  It became evident that there were two different kinds of consumers for the brand, each with very different expectations. A decision would have to be made about where to place the communications emphasis: dry skin prevention and restoration or softer, moisturized skin. Contrary to conventional wisdom, the advertising strategy and executions focused on both benefits, with notable success.

Verbal cues casually dropped by the respondent during the course of an interview can open up fresh areas of insight. In one study, while observers watched people cleaning the bathroom, they heard many use the word or a variation of *shiny*. Respondents spoke of shining up the tub or the toilet or pointed with pride to a shiny sink. Probing what they meant, researchers found that *shine* was a synonym for *cleanliness*. If a bathroom surface was shiny, it was assumed to be clean. Furthermore, in many respondents' minds, a shiny surface also meant a disinfected surface—one free of germs. This discovery was just the kind of insight needed for advertising executions and other forms of consumer communication.

FIGURE 6.4

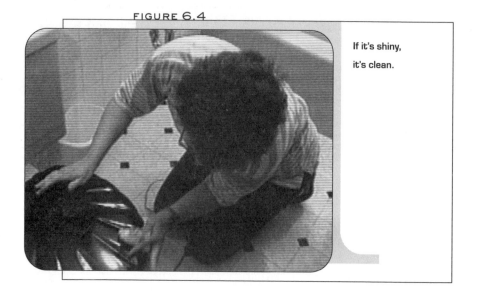

If it's shiny,
it's clean.

Exploration and Adventure

In-home observation provides the time and the familiar environment for following up on verbal and visual leads. The interviewer can afford to be relentless (but nicely so) once she scents a hot, unexplored trail. In fact, sometimes these trails may take up most of the interview time, if they're particularly exciting. Often it's the exploration of all the twists and turns of an issue that leads to a big, panoramic idea, and the researcher should have the courage and the smarts to depart from and even disregard the interview guide if and when the trail is hot enough.

It's important for the people funding the research to accept an interview deviating from the plan and to think of observational research as one part information gathering, one part getting an intimate feel for the consumer, and one part adventure. They should be ready and eager for new discoveries and surprise. If it's by-the-numbers research they want, then they should buy some other kind of study.

In the Bathroom

There is almost nothing most respondents will refuse to do in front of an observer, if they are presented with the idea in the right way. Observational researchers have been invited into bathrooms all over America often early in the morning to watch consumers floss, brush their teeth, apply skin lotion, wash their hands, shampoo, set their hair, clean their toilets, and even take a shower.

Why do they do it? Why do almost 80 percent of those asked to be part of an interview—even in the bathroom—accept? They're not kooks, weirdos or some kind of perverse exhibitionists but normal, everyday people who fit the specs.

A good recruiter, working from a well-written screener, will make the interview sound like fun and assure the prospective respondent that the request for an interview comes from an established, reputable company and that respondents' privacy will be respected. They explain that the interview is in the interest of a good cause—better products. And there's nothing like the inducement of a fee to clinch an appointment.

Although the bathroom may be small, it is an ideal place to interview. The fact that the room is the place where the consumer focuses on his or her body parts fosters a direct, honest attitude, and mitigates the tendency for the respondent to "take the stage." It's difficult for respondents to be anything but themselves when applying an underarm deodorant or when there's toothpaste foam dribbling out of their mouths. It also helps if you ask respondents to wear—within reason—what they usually wear when they shave or brush their teeth or set their hair. And getting them to describe to you what they're doing as they do it keeps them open and communicating.

What do you do if the project involves a bath or shower soap? You get as close as possible to the bath or shower experience, asking respondents to wear a bathing suit while they bathe.

What can you discover by watching and interviewing consumers as they perform their personal care regimens? For one thing, you will learn the role and significance (or insignificance) of your product and product category within the various routines people put themselves through every morning and evening. Is your toothbrush the first thing they use? How much time do they spend brushing their teeth compared with the time they devote to other parts of the oral hygiene regimen? Is the handle hard to manipulate? Is it difficult for respondents to reach their back teeth? Do they know what brand of brush they're using? (Most don't know.) Is it the same brand as their toothpaste? Where do they store their toothbrush? If you happen to manufacture toothbrushes, answers to questions like these could affect both the design and the marketing of your product.

- A few years ago, by videotaping respondents applying the prototype of an antiperspirant and deodorant with a new kind of applicator, observational researchers made a simple discovery just before the product was due in the test market. Many consumers trying to use the product couldn't get to first base. They couldn't get the antiperspirant/deodorant to come out of the new applicator. Neither R&D nor the marketing and sales departments had caught the problem. The prototype was sent back to the lab, and the company saved many hundreds of thousands of dollars in test market costs.

- Personal revelations come easily to consumers' lips when they're in the bathroom. Interviewing respondents as they cleaned their bathrooms, researchers heard a surprising admission from a well-educated young woman. She had spent over twenty minutes cleaning the tiles above the bathtub. When asked what the reward was, she confessed that she did it mainly for her husband's approval—a confession you might have expected four decades ago, but not from a young person today. A few others in the study admitted similar motivations. Could we be witnessing an embryonic retro trend?

- Taking note of seniors' bathrooms, observers found a high preponderance of antibacterial liquid hand soap. Probing for the reason, the research team discovered an unusually high fear of germs in this age group. Some senior respondents, especially women, washed their hands twelve to fifteen times a day. And many wouldn't dream of washing with anything but an antibacterial soap.

In most houses there are two cores, and one of them is the bathroom. It's where most of the personal relationships between individual members of the family and products take place.

IN THE KITCHEN

In the kitchen, individuals relate to products as part of a family unit. The pantry and the refrigerator hold products bought, organized, dispensed, and monitored for the sake of the family—unless, of course, the respondent is single. The observer will find in the kitchen and dining areas a gold mine for product-related family interaction. Food and food-related products and situations, as any psychologist can tell you, carry some pretty weighty emotional baggage.

Not long ago, researchers visited families in various areas of the United States to understand consumers' reactions to a newly introduced Italian pasta. One of the researchers' interesting discoveries was that pasta brought families together. Kids and adults couldn't resist hanging around the kitchen to watch the pasta and wait for it to finish cooking. Often, family members were enlisted to test whether it was done. With lots of fun and mutual kidding, they'd pull a strand out of the boiling water and squeeze it, chomp on it, cut it, or even throw it against the cabinet to see if it stuck (the old country way of testing whether it was *al dente*). And when it came time to eat, even the most restrained families found it hard to maintain a subdued decorum over a plate of fettucine and pasta sauce.

Potato chips, on the other hand, frequently brought out family competition. No matter how many chips were poured into the bowl at the start of the family dinner, the younger members of the family would fight for the remaining chips.

But for bringing out family politics, potato chips can't compare to cold cereal. Anyone who has ever observed parents and young children selecting breakfast cereal has seen the war between nutritional value and sugar content. The negotiations can go on for quite some time, usually ending with the adult compromising his or her principles. (As long as he eats something.) But she will come back to the fray with another nourishing cereal he just might like this time. In one observational study, a boy pulled out eight different cereal boxes from the cabinet for the researcher—each depleted by one bowlfull.

FIGURE 6.5

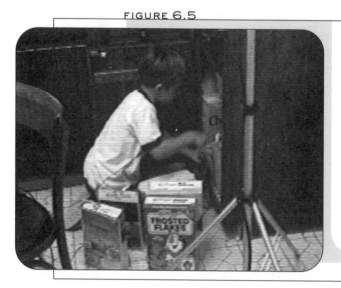

He's tried each of these cereals—once.

How should one observe in the kitchen or around the dining table? If the interviewer has successfully ingratiated herself with the respondent, he or she can stand and watch while the meal is being prepared, like a friend who dropped by to chat at the end of the day. Here, particularly, a female interviewer will usually encourage more natural actions and responses, especially if the meal preparer is a woman. Questions and conversation should flow directly from whatever the respondent is doing at the moment—whether cutting up the carrots or opening a heat-and-serve package of meat sauce.

Whether the researcher's record consists of notes, a still picture or videotape, every action related to the product and issues involved should be noted: whether and how well respondents read directions, the trouble they have opening the package, the way the contents are poured into the pan, whether they stir the food, whether they combine it with other ingredients, whether they test it, how they serve it. The smallest actions sometimes have a way of being the most relevant—if not for positioning or advertising executions, then for product or package modification.

AT THE TABLE

Some researchers find that sitting along with the family at the table while they eat the meal works best. They share the meal and become part of the ebb and flow of passing the food, eating, and talking. Questions are posed casually, as if they are part of the day-to-day family conversation. More formal questioning is postponed until the end of the meal or at least the end of the course.

Others feel that sitting at the table makes them more like company and will result in the conversation being somewhat restrained. They prefer to observe unobtrusively, slightly away from the table, noting the action and saving questions until later.

Either way, it's equally important to listen and to watch what happens. What's put out on the table? Butter? Salt? Ketchup? Mustard? Other condiments? How are they used? What liquids are served? Did the daughter leave her french fries for last? Remember to ask why. And what was that sour expression that passed over Dad's face when he drank the juice? Why did the eight-year-old put ketchup on his string beans? Maybe there's a product idea there. Does everyone finish his or her plate? Does anyone reach for seconds? Are there leftovers? What happens to them? Is it hard to clean up after the meal? Watch to see who actually does the cleaning. (The cleanup chore could be an impediment to future purchase.)

Don't leave the kitchen without examining the storage areas, pantry, and refrigerator. In a recent project, it was observed that many beverages were kept in the storage areas and pantries of the respondents interviewed, but few examples of the studied beverage were kept there. Yet, this same beverage was very prominent in their refrigerators. Attempting to resolve this discrepancy pointed the way to increase consumer consumption of the brand.

Where you find the product often will tell you what the respondent really thinks about it far better than words can. Is the beverage refrigerated among the staples used every day—the milk, the orange juice? Or is it placed among the indulgence products—the wine or beer? Are you studying canned vegetables? How many different cans are in the pantry? Is there a full range of canned vegetables? Or are they grouped together with canned hash and other canned meats? If so, it may mean the cans are used as a standby. The ensuing marketing strategy will vary depending on whether the brand is used regularly or on a standby basis.

Home Cleaning

Cleaning the house and its immediate environment presents many opportunities for observational research. In the process of doing each room and the yard people may use a dozen cleaning products and at least as many tools and appliances. As I am writing this chapter in my home office, the house cleaner is working in other parts of the apartment. I count eleven different substances she uses to clean the surfaces and do the laundry. And I am not including dish-washing supplies.

Research of all kinds tells us that consumers are cleaning less and they're less concerned about a little mess or a little dirt showing here and there because they have less time these days. Observational research applied to house cleaning is ideal for testing time- and effort-saving product ideas, modifications, and positioning. That's why Clean Shower became an overnight success and why 2000 Flushes has been so popular.

Research using videotape is particularly effective in finding unfulfilled gaps in each cleaning category. It is also useful in uncovering those small differences among product attributes that may be linked to a significant benefit—or to a negative consumer reaction.

One study of bathroom cleaners revealed that consumers reacted negatively to a product that was clearly superior in its category. On the early videotapes, they were seen to wrinkle their noses when they were asked to open the bottle and use the cleanser. In later interviews, consumers were questioned about their reaction. They explained that the harsh, acidic smell emanating from the cleanser when it was opened made them think the product might be unsafe to use in a bathroom frequented by children. Because the product truly was safe, it was a simple matter to add a pleasing aroma that modified the harshness.

What prompts a person to do the laundry? Is it her family's overflowing clothes hampers, or does she wash their clothes every Monday, no matter what? What's the usual laundry ritual? How long does it take from the time the first load is put into the washer until the last sheet is folded and put away? Is there any way to shorten the time, to cut down on the effort? Studying the laundry routine via observational research will give you plenty of new product or product modification ideas. And, just like the detergent study mentioned at the beginning of this book, it might turn up a whole new way to say *clean* or *fresh* or *soft*.

Washing the dishes—whether by hand or machine—is a fruitful area for observation. Whether consumers put dish-washing liquid directly on the sponge or squirt it into the basin directly affects the rate at which the product is used up. Is your product used when consumers wash their hands at the kitchen sink, or is it considered too harsh? Do respondents use their dish-washing liquid to clean other surfaces? If so, would that lead to the marketing of a single, all-purpose product for every use in the kitchen—including washing dishes?

The habits and practices of consumers loading dishwashers are of significant interest to manufacturers of dishwashers as well as to those who make dishwasher detergents. When is the dishwasher considered full enough to start? How much detergent do people actually use? Do they follow package or dishwasher instructions? Can the glasses and cups be racked securely? Is there enough room for a day's worth of dishes? How do they judge cleanliness? Are there times they prefer to wash dishes by hand rather than by machine? When and why? Being right there, recording consumers as they do the dishes, will give you insights into what actually happens and its marketing implications.

How do consumers clean surfaces such as floors? What are the problems they have when they vacuum? Watching these processes will provide valuable insights for the manufacturer of all-purpose cleansers, sponges, and vacuum cleaners. It may even give rise to product modifications in accord with today's habits and practices.

What do family members responsible for cleaning the house want? A number of respondents have said in so many words, "If only I could just wave a magic wand and everything in the house would suddenly be clean." But, especially in an era in which some women are making the decision to stay home with a child after a relatively short working career, products need to give consumers a sense that they are responsible for or in control of the home environment, that they are doing something to improve or at least maintain it. Most women we have studied who clean their homes—even those who work as well as keep house—have a need to feel they are accomplishing something beyond speed and convenience. A completely hands-off cleaning product may not be acceptable to some consumers.

HOME IMPROVEMENT

Observational research offers a cornucopia of insights when it comes to home maintenance. Do-it-yourself processes like laying down tiles, painting rooms, adding a closet, mowing the lawn, weeding and fertilizing, and waterproofing a deck or staining a piece of furniture can be time-consuming and frustrating. What are the elements of the process that drive people up the wall? How can they be simplified? Do the instructions need to be made clearer? Observational research can provide a complete time and motion study of consumers engaged in a process on their own turf. And it can find new methods of application and new product ideas that can make home maintenance tasks easier and more fun.

What are the major satisfactions experienced by home owners performing maintenance or making improvements? Do they enjoy the process more than the end result or vice versa? Don't just ask the question. Take pictures or videotape their faces while they work.

THE PACKAGE

A vital use for observation research is in uncovering problems and opportunities associated with your package. Is it easy to open? Can the contents be accessed easily? How well does it reseal? Is your package too large for storage? Are the directions on the back readable? How could your package be improved? Observational research will give you the answers.

Here, too, the videotape methodology is particularly useful. By filming consumers handling your package—from opening to disposal—you'll make a complete record of every trouble spot and create the opportunity for discovering how to fix the problems.

When observing hearing aid users as they examined a compact, plastic battery container, researchers saw them respond quite favorably. The plastic package would protect the hearing aid batteries and fit easily into pocketbooks or shirt pockets. Nevertheless, they kept turning the container over and over in their hands. How did the darn thing open? They couldn't figure it out. The researcher finally had to show them how to open the package. Clearly, an improvement was needed. Respondents gave suggestions freely for other ways the batteries could be carried.

Middle-aged and older toothpaste users did not like the idea that they couldn't get all the paste out of a tube. The new plastic tubes could not be squeezed and rolled up like the old metal ones they remembered. Videotapes revealed consumers using clamps, pressing their fists against the tube, and sometimes cutting the tube open to get at the remaining paste.

FIGURE 6.6

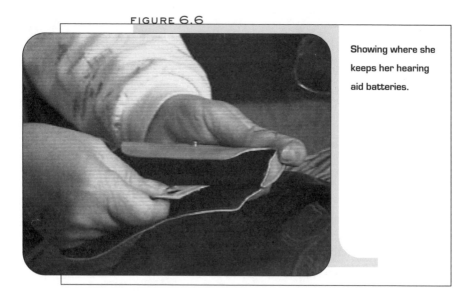

Showing where she keeps her hearing aid batteries.

An observational researcher may pinpoint package improvement needs missed by even the sharpest R&D person. Like most human beings who stare at the same object day after day, an R&D man or woman, no matter how perspicacious, will sometimes take a glitch, gap, or flaw for granted. A trained observational researcher coming to the product fresh and seeing it in actual use will often spot the consumer's slightest trouble with the product, trouble that could lead to a significant marketable improvement.

WHAT THIS CHAPTER TELLS YOU

- An observational interview is different from any other kind of interview.

- Observational researchers explore every aspect of a consumer's life that touches your product.

- Observational researchers are in the bathroom early in the morning.

- Observational researchers join the family in the kitchen and at the table.

- They're right there along with the consumer when the floor gets mopped, the lawn gets mowed, or the house gets painted.

- Observational researchers look for—and find—trouble when consumers open your package.

- Observational research generates reality-based product ideas, modifications, and improvements.

7

WATCHING CONSUMERS SHOP:

IN-STORE OBSERVATION PUTS YOU RIGHT THERE WHEN CONSUMERS SELECT— OR REJECT—YOUR PRODUCT

Observing the shopping experience is different in many ways from the in-home experience. The venue is not as private, and there are time constraints.

OBSERVING SHOPPERS SELECT GENERAL MERCHANDISE

A number of observational researchers include supermarkets, mass merchandisers, and large drugstores in their work. If your interest lies in how consumers shop, you need to consider some factors before the project begins.

Types of In-Store Research

There are a few ways in-store research is usually performed. One way is to recruit shoppers beforehand and follow them around the store while they select the products they want and put them in their grocery baskets, interviewing them throughout. Another way is to watch shoppers either surreptitiously or on a monitor as they select from a specific shelf and then approach them for a brief interview (for an incentive of course).

If shoppers are prerecruited and followed around, there'll be as much time as needed for the interview. And you will find out what departments of the store the shopper visits first and second and third. But you may not see some of the natural hesitations and fumbling package examinations you might see when respondents feel no one is watching. (The supermarket is not as familiar an environment as the home.)

FIGURE 7.1

Following a shopper through the aisle gives the researcher more time to interview them.

On the other hand, after watching from a hidden position, although you have had a chance to observe the real shopper and all of his or her real reactions, you now have at best fifteen minutes to find out why they did what they did—no matter how much you offer as an incentive. Time is even more precious than money to many people. Unless they've planned beforehand to give you their time, you can forget getting more than fifteen minutes from people at the store. In addition, the information you glean from the interview will be related mainly to only one product category.

FIGURE 7.2

While the researcher watches from a hidden position, this shopper climbs the shelves.

There's one more option. You may want to consider dividing up your project, using some prerecruited respondents and some approached at random.

Store Access

Store access is generally arranged through the sales department of the manufacturer funding the study. This may take a few weeks, involving the local and regional retail chains of command. And it may take a bit of prompting. So allow enough time.

Obtainable Information

Here are a few excerpts from actual interviews taken from an in-store observation of juice beverage shoppers in large supermarkets at various locations. The material was recorded right at the shelf. First, the shoppers were filmed with a hidden camera and, second, the same shoppers were interviewed in front of an open camera. The excerpts are included here to show you the kind of information you can expect to obtain from random in-store interviews. The numbers represent codes differentiating the interview portion.

CLIMBS UP SHELF TO GET CAPRI SUN.

MIS 5:23:00
SHOWS TWO 8-PACK BOXES OF CAPRI SUN RED BERRY AND WILD CHERRY.

MIS 5:23:15
My three kids drink them. Ages 15, 11, and 7. They ask for flavors, make me write it down.

MIT 6:30:40
I know my daughter likes the punch flavor.
DAUGHTER SHOWS BOXES.

MIS 1:12:13
The Juicy Juice boxes

MIS 1:12:28
Plan to buy this specific one? Not this specific one.

DISS TO MIS 1:12:38
What made you select this particular one? She grabbed it. Grabs it all the time.

FATHER AND SON

NJ S2:17:10
I let him decide what juice, because I'll buy juice and he won't drink it. I know he'll drink apple—his favorite. He likes Juicy Juice and Mott's.

MITC2 CAM.1 T4:53:25
MOTHER AND DAUGHTER LOOK THROUGH BOXES FOR
FLAVORS.

MIT6:04:00
Daughter: *I look for flavor.*

MIT6:07:00
Mother: *We look for juices. Fun juices. Whatever
appeals to them.*

MIT5:25:32
To Daughter: *I saw you're the one that actually selected
it. How did you select it?*
Daughter: *I don't know, it looked good.*

T5:25:44
*I had Mott's before, and I decided to try a different
flavor.*

T5:26:54
To Mother: *How do you decide? Generally, whatever
she likes.*

These particular sequences reveal the strong influence of
kids in the selection of juice beverages. As many in-store studies do, this one uncovered proprietary information that has
helped the beverage manufacturer who sponsored it enhance
marketing and packaging practices.

No matter which way you decide to explore the in-store
experience, you will almost always glean valuable information
and insight. The hierarchy of motivation can be learned with
some accuracy: what people look for primarily, secondarily, and
thirdly when they go shopping. What's more important? The
brand? The category? The flavor? The price? Did the shopper see
an ad or a promotion for the product? You also can discover if
your product is difficult to find, is put in the shade by other
brands, or is just seldom noticed by consumers shopping the
category.

- In an in-store study, shoppers were observed hunting high and low for a well-known brand of single-use cameras in a giant West Coast drugstore. When they finally found what they were looking for, it was locked up in a glass case, and they had to ask the clerk to open the case for them.

- In another study, shopper after shopper in a supermarket passed by a new, well-advertised category of concentrated beverages. Interviews at the shelf revealed that shoppers remembered the advertising but were not connecting it to the display on the shelf.

Do shoppers buy mainly on sale? You'll find that out in the store. Are they discouraged from buying your product by some-one else's new brand or bright package? How much do kids or other family members influence their choice? You'll discover that, too.

What do shoppers do when the product they want isn't there? Do they choose a substitute or go to another store? And who hears their anger or annoyance over the inconvenience—the store or the manufacturer? You'll get an earful.

Whether you're interviewing for ten minutes or for a longer time as your respondent shops, you will learn how and when the shopper plans to use the product and why it happens to be on the shopping list today (assuming there is a list) Is it a replacement or an addition? Did someone in the family ask for it? Did the shopper see an ad or commercial for the brand? Or is the choice motivated by a coupon or a sale featured in the store flyer?

Unlike in-home studies, where there is more time for in-depth probing and longer, richer responses, the methodology of following a consumer through a shopping trip is liable to elicit quicker, more distracted answers to the interviewer's questions. It is wise to interview a larger number of consumers for in-store studies. A minimum of forty respondents is necessary to discern a pattern and to understand how the consumer shops for a par-ticular brand.

The retailer along with the manufacturer—regardless of what the store is selling—can benefit from in-store observational research. Housecalls has yet to complete an in-store assignment for a manufacturer without the retailer asking for the findings as well. The large supermarket, mass merchandiser, and drug- or department store can benefit from studying what customers do in specific aisles or within individual store departments.

> The shopping experience will tell you how and why the consumer selects a brand on a particular day. It will not tell you how and why the consumer lives with that brand on an ongoing basis.

For a complete picture of purchase motivations and actual usage patterns, the ideal observational research strategy is a series of in-home interviews coupled with in-store interviews— if possible with the same people. (If you do decide to have a combined research project performed with the same people, pre-recruit them and follow them around behind their shopping carts.) Such a study gives you a picture of purchase, usage, and consumer-product relationship in complete detail. It may turn up a few surprises, too. For example, people may select your product at the shelf for one reason and use it at home for an entirely different reason. Likewise, a product targeted to and purchased for a child may be consumed by someone of an entirely different age when it gets home.

Observing Consumers in Specialty Stores or Departments

The next few pages contain some department and specialty store examples of observational research in action—including suggestions of ways in which observational research can be valuable to both retailers and manufacturers. These examples can be applied to most classes of retailing.

Clothing Stores

The shopping experience is a good opportunity to examine the hierarchy of purchase motivations in the fashion industry—a hierarchy that has not received the kind of attention researchers have paid to purchase motivations in other product categories. Ask a trained observer to accompany people as they shop for clothing. Have them watch carefully while customers browse through the racks or examine the garments the salesperson brings them and especially while they try on clothing items in front of the mirror.

The process of elimination as a shopper begins to select may tell you as much about his or her real reasons for purchase as the garment that is finally chosen. Asked why she returned an item of clothing to the rack, she may explain that it's the wrong style, color or price. Or she may have a negative feeling about the label. Or the item may not fit her idea of contemporary clothing. Or it may not go with something she's thinking of wearing it with. The answer may also be, "It just isn't me," which raises the question of personal identity as expressed through clothes.

I had a valuable experience watching the body language of a number of men trying on suits in front of the mirror in a New York department store. Observing the stance of each person, I realized there was a subtle but decided shift in the way they held themselves just as they stepped up to the mirror. The stance became more pronounced than it had been a few seconds before. After watching the fourth or fifth man, it came to me—I was witnessing what the garment does, not just *for* but *to* the customer. Consciously or unconsciously, almost everyone in this situation was asking the same question: "Who am I now? What does this clothing make me look like—to others and to myself?"

When shoppers tried on an item that was in accord with the image they thought they projected or wanted to project, they became somebody—or at least more of the somebody they believed or wanted themselves to be.

Either during or after the trying-on experience, it is useful to probe in depth the consumer's self-image as expressed through the clothing he or she has selected. I was able to do so after I watched a thirty-five-year-old man pull his shirt cuffs out of the suit jacket he was trying on, smooth out his tie, throw his shoulders back, and turn slightly in profile while gazing approvingly at the mirror. As he stepped away, I told him he looked great in the suit he was trying on. He dropped the posture and responded instantly by telling me the price and showing me the label. (It was a very expensive suit.) He explained that in his business he had to look like Wall Street—even though his business had nothing to do with securities. Clearly, the suit made him feel like a highly affluent stockbroker. It was a fantasy come to life and his main reason for buying it.

This kind of probing is reflected in women's fashion advertising, but it has not been performed enough in the category of men's fashion. I suspect that any researcher observing men trying on suits, for example, would find a range of images that almost any kind of clothing confers on the wearer—from a Beverly Hills look to the solid, traditional image of old money, from casual to formal wear, images that can be used to great effect in men's fashion advertising especially now that many firms have expanded dress-down Fridays to the entire week. Casual wear is a break from the uniform and almost demands self-expression.

> Clothing is theater—for men as well as for women. Manufacturers of both men's suits and men's casual wear have an unexploited opportunity to observe and develop positioning in accord with their customers' personal postures and fantasies.

Clearly, the same kinds of observations can't be made when consumers buy clothing from an E-commerce website. But, watching them at the computer can tell you a lot about the selection process.

Home Furnishing Stores

The process of making a decision about major items of furniture can be agonizing particularly for young people who are doing it the first time. Looking at a two-thousand-dollar sofa or even a less expensive chair, shoppers will think first yes, then no, and then maybe—generally driving furniture salespeople up the wall.

People of any age who buy for their homes do not always understand their own needs and motivations and what drives their decisions. Is the prime mover taste? Function? Price? What's in? The name and reputation of the store or manufacturer? Getting a full understanding of the selection process for its market segment would be of enormous help to a furniture maker or retailer.

An observational researcher, tagging along with shoppers from the day they make the decision to replace or add an item of furniture through the search and right on to the final choice, depth interviewing at every stage, can provide an eye-opening understanding of shopping and make both the buying and selling efforts more efficient. Researchers may find, for example, that one of the factors standing in the way of a quicker decision is the inability of many people to visualize how a piece of furniture would look in the available space. If so, it's not difficult for today's technology to provide the means of visualizing the furniture where it would sit in the customer's home.

Observational researchers may notice among their subjects a frequent reference to celebrities, and the ways they furnish their homes. Point-of-sale material concerning the styles of furniture currently favored by selected celebrities may be just what is needed to close the sale.

Depending on the customer base, researchers may uncover a primary concern with quality and sturdiness—particularly after consumers have purchased furniture elsewhere that then fell apart. In such cases it may be wise to prominently feature warranties and guarantees.

Record the actual retail experience on videotape. What is the behavior of prospective buyers from the moment they walk into the store until the moment they leave (with or without having made a purchase)? To where are the customers' eyes pulled? How do they examine an item of furniture? What questions do they ask the salespeople? How long do they spend in the store before deciding?

These questions have been raised—and answered—by observational studies in supermarkets. Such studies can provide valuable data to a home-furnishings retailer, making the store layout as well as the selling and marketing process more effective.

Electronics Stores

Wander into your neighborhood electronics store, a branch of a national chain, and there are three questions you may not be able to answer for the next few minutes:

- Where do they keep what I'm looking for?

- Is there anyone around who can help me?

- Can I try a store model?

Improving the purchase process is the name of the game—for both the manufacturer and the retailer of electronic equipment. And that means helping the customer find and select more quickly and efficiently what he or she wants, or should want.

For a retailer, one of the key questions concerning the purchase of a computer, printer, fax machine, TV set, videotape recorder, or cell phone is "Does the shopper know what he or she wants before entering the store?" Particularly if shoppers know the category but not the brand or model or if they're just browsing, observational research can be highly productive for store management.

Where in the store do browsers go first? What attracts them and what do they ignore? At what point does the shopper start to examine the merchandise, look at prices, or actually try a piece of equipment? How long after entering the store does the shopper ask a salesperson for directions to a particular section or ask about a specific item of merchandise? What is the influence of point-of-sale material on the purchaser and on the browser? Observational research findings can also help the sales staff develop a better instinct for precisely at what point to approach customers and ask if they need any assistance.

For a manufacturer of electronic equipment, knowing what attracts undecided buyers to its brand or to a competitor in the store aisles can be very valuable. It may lead to a change in packaging—either to clarify information or to make the product more compelling. Observational research can also tell a manufacturer what's right or wrong with the point-of-sale and promotional material it offers the retailer and how to improve it.

Recently, a manufacturer of printers, copiers, and other electronic equipment used an observational research company to deploy hidden cameras overlooking the aisles of an electronics store and to perform exit interviews among both purchasers and nonpurchasers. The purpose was to determine the effect on current and potential customers of proposed in-store promotional material. Did the proposed flyers, carton designs, and display material improve the company's presence in the stores? Did they make it easier for the purchaser to find what he or she wanted? Did they do a better job of attracting the browser to the company's products?

As of this writing, the findings have not yet been compiled. But, assuming the results are definitive, both the manufacturer and the retailer can take immediate steps to make it easier for customers to find exactly what they're looking for, to provide more opportunities for them to examine the merchandise, and to use point-of-sale material more effectively for their mutual benefit.

Fast-Food Restaurants

Once you get hungry consumers inside a Burger King, Wendy's or McDonald's, the name of the game is customer satisfaction, which involves more than the quality of the food. How easily do consumers make their selections? Are there enough choices available? Is there any confusion concerning the listings? How long do consumers have to wait in line? After they buy their food, can they easily access the tables? Are the tables clean? How do consumers respond to in-restaurant promotions? Do they believe they're having a tasty, satisfying, nourishing meal at a fair price?

Whether you're a store manager or an executive for a fast-food chain, these are questions you probably ask yourself. The answers are vital for your business, yet as is true for most of us who find ourselves in the same environment day after day, it is very easy to get used to and overlook certain aspects of your business that may be obvious to a trained observer.

Observational research can make an organized record of what your customers do and think from the instant they walk in until the moment they dump their trays into the waste bin. The recording process can go on for days, giving you a broad spectrum of customer behavior and attitude. It can include on-the-spot interviews with customers at the table. If the record is kept on videotape, you can return to it again and again, just as your observational research company will do, to study and analyze it, and to arrive at consumer-generated ways to improve your business. Once you have acted on the findings, making the improvements the research had suggested, you might want to do a follow-up study in the same restaurants to see if the improvements have raised the level of customer satisfaction and to understand what makes successful innovations work so you can expand on them.

Observing Salespeople

If you're involved with retail marketing, you will want to know how your salespeople handle your customers. Are they attentive, knowledgeable, helpful to customers? Do they reflect the mission and the image of the store? What can the salespeople do to improve customer relations?

Observational research can help you find the answers to these questions. Watching, listening, and shopping like other customers, setting up situations that put salespeople to the test, and interviewing the salespeople directly, the observational researcher will make a record of transactions and words spoken and then perform an analysis.

At some point in the research, it pays to ask the salespeople their opinions of the issues discovered when the researchers were observing and probing customers. Salespeople are there on the floor, day in and day out, and they will have observed customer behavior at their stores far longer than either you or your researcher have. What they've seen and what they think is highly significant.

However, remember that salespeople's opinions may not be the most objective. They are not trained observers, and all salespeople I have ever met have their own axes to grind. Nevertheless, they can shed much light on the purchase process. They are not to be overlooked.

Street-Corner Interviews

"The man on the street" has held an almost mystical attraction for advertising and marketing people. While writing this book, I've received requests from two different advertising agencies to find out what the "man on the street" thinks. The agencies wanted a researcher with a video camera to stop people at random on a busy city street and ask them what they think about certain product issues.

Whenever I hear such requests, I always question if the requested research has anything to do with the location of the interview, the clothes potential respondents might be wearing, or something they might be carrying—such as a newspaper. If it doesn't relate to a specific attribute, the most such research will yield is a collection of generic sound bites on camera, the same kinds of sound bites you hear and see on your local six o'clock news program: "Yeah, we're all going to miss Michael Jordan" or "I think they should lock them up and throw away the key."

For a street-corner interview to be valid and to count as real research, it should have something to do with the activity the respondent is directly involved with at the moment. For example, recently an interviewer and a cameraperson stationed themselves on the street outside a restaurant and interviewed patrons leaving the premises concerning their satisfaction with the service and the meal. The results proved highly useful to the restaurant client.

Sometimes this same kind of research takes place in the lobby of a movie theater when the show lets out or in the station where commuters come off the train. If the research concerns the movie or the commuter service the respondents just experienced, the random interviews can have weight and meaning.

Street-corner interviews also can work if they have to do with a specific style or brand of clothing people are wearing such as a current clothing trend or a certain brand of sneaker. And street-corner interviews can be meaningful when they involve people in a mall who are carrying a shopping bag from a certain store. A few questions about the shopping experience in that store are likely to turn up some useful answers.

But if the random, street-corner interviews you're contemplating have nothing to do with anything the respondent is involved with at the moment, save your money. Telephone interviews are cheaper, and they'll give you the same kind of generic information.

What This Chapter Tells You

- Observational research can show you—right at the point of sale—the primary, secondary, and other motivations that prompt your consumer to select your brand.

- The motivations can be observed not only in supermarkets, mass merchandisers, and drugstores, but also at specialty stores that sell clothing, electronics, furniture, or other goods.

- Observational research can show you how to increase customer satisfaction at fast-food restaurants.

- You will discover from observational research what role—if any—your sales promotion and advertising play in the actual selection of items and of retail outlets.

- Observational research reveals what store traffic patterns and displays attract customers to specific areas and merchandise. Both the retailer and the manufacturer benefit.

- Observational research can tell you what part your salespeople play or don't play in the purchase process.

8

OBSERVING CONSUMERS IN MOTION:

ON THE ROAD, IN THE AIR,

AND IN CYBERSPACE

People in their own personal space—either virtual or real— act and respond to products differently than when they are with others. More and more, observational research is making actionable discoveries about the consumer relationship with cars and other forms of travel and to consumers' increasingly complex journeys through the Internet.

THE CAR-DRIVER RELATIONSHIP

For research and development purposes, car manufacturers have used still and motion picture cameras for years to watch the way a new model functions around the test track. Only recently have they started to employ observational research to understand the relationship between car and driver.

Respondents' relationships to their cars can offer a multitude of insights—on both the psychological and physical levels. Just the way people approach their cars as they're about to unlock them can tell you volumes. Do they walk around their cars, inspecting them for imperfections that may have happened since the last time they drove? Do they pause almost imperceptibly for an admiring glance? Or do they slightly purse their lips, akin to girding of the loins, in preparation for yet another problem with their vehicles? Some people just get in and drive off without so much as an eye blink. Whatever they do on the approach will be a strong clue as to what their cars mean in their lives. It will provide a good take-off point to the researcher for later verbal probing.

In the last few years, car manufacturers have learned a lot about how to improve car design by putting a video camera in the front seat and videotaping the driver on an entire commuting or shopping trip. How do drivers handle the controls? Are the controls well placed? Are they easy or difficult to use? Watch the expressions on drivers' faces as they manipulate the car through traffic and park. What frustrates them? What annoys them? Are there blind spots that might cause safety problems or that make parking harder than it should be? Do drivers have to take their eyes off the road for any length of time to read the gauges on the dashboard or use the radio? Do they have to crane their necks to see if they're going to fit into that tight space at the curb?

Loading the car, either with people or packages, is a natural study for observational research. Is there enough room for the family—in the front and the back? Is the vehicle easy to get in and out of? Does the trunk or rear portion of the minivan provide problem-free access for grocery bags and other supplies?

Just the basic knowledge of where a driver takes his or her car each day—the kind of traffic, the length of the trips, the frequency of loading and unloading—can be highly useful to car makers designing and marketing cars for specific consumer segments. It's a good idea either to have an interviewer riding along with the driver or to take the time afterward to go over the footage with the driver. The interviewer should probe in detail why the driver does what he or she does. At the same time, the interviewer can investigate the relationship between car and driver.

The car-driver relationship is perhaps somewhat more complex than in the 1950s, when Dr. Ernest Dichter blazed across the research universe with his concept of motivation research. Among the ideas he developed that were successfully employed by the advertising industry at that time was the concept (albeit sexist by our standards today) that, on a symbolic level, a convertible was a man's mistress, and a station wagon represented a man's wife. The percentage of women owning cars has since jumped enormously, and the market for cars has fragmented into many different buying segments—from sport utility vehicles to family-centered minivans to sedate luxury sedans to jazzy, sporty two-seaters for younger buyers. Dichter would have to add significantly to his categorizations for them to be relevant to today's population of car owners.

The observational researcher can tap into many kinds of meaning—especially in a one-on-one conversation in the intimate, private space of a respondent's automobile. Questioning both indirectly and directly, a research should be able to explore issues of status, personal identity, power, freedom, and more as they touch on car ownership. Are these motivations as much of a driving force (forgive the pun) for a leased car as they are for a car that's owned? This is an interesting question for both a car manufacturer and a dealer's association.

There is also a wealth of meaning in the way a car is displayed—or not displayed—when it's not being used. Is it parked in the driveway, close to the road so that the neighbors and passersby can see it? Or is it kept within the protection (or secrecy) of a garage? How often is it washed? How often is it tuned up? Is the inside clean and relatively free of junk? More than a simple matter of pride, the display and condition of the car reveals something of the way the owner feels about himself or herself and about his or her readiness for the next automobile purchase.

An area that has yet to be explored observationally—at this writing—is what goes on in the dealership during the car-buying process. It would be fascinating to videotape the stroke-by-stroke negotiations in an auto salesperson's cubicle. Watching and listening with one camera trained on the buyer and another on the salesperson would point out effective and ineffective selling and negotiating techniques and provide the basis for a training video for dealerships, dealer associations, and car manufacturers.

Another area worthy of exploration is the search for a car deal on the Internet. It would be interesting to know how Internet shopping affects the car-buying process. How much of the buyer's decision is made in front of the computer? How much is made when he or she visits the dealership? Following an on-line shopper through the entire search and buying process would point out ways the marketing process—particularly on a local level—can be made more efficient.

Exploration of the car-driver relationship via observational research has perhaps gone beyond scratching the surface—but there's an opportunity to delve deeper. The automobile is such an important part of our lives and our economy, yet we know more about consumers' intimate, personal relationships to their bathroom sponges than we do about their relationships to their cars.

PEOPLE AND THEIR COMPUTERS

During the last few years, anthropologists from various universities have begun to study the computer user in minute detail. In fact, according to Dr. Susan Squires, president-elect of the National Association for the Practice of Anthropology (*The New York Times*, June 10, 1999) the high-tech arena, with its intense pressure and high rate of product failures, has become most popular for anthropological study. In the same article, Dr. Marietta Baba, chairwoman of the Anthropology Department at Wayne State University, indicated that close-up studies of movement skills have helped in the design of the computer mouse, joystick, and touch screen. The mouse, for example, lets the hand mimic the way the eyes scan a computer screen.

There are a number of computer-related consumer experiences in which observational research can be useful: setting up a new computer (known as the *out-of-the-box experience*), installing and learning new software, using a website, and buying on-line. The first of these—setting up a new computer at home—can be a real pain in the neck, not to mention other parts of the anatomy. There are those amazing people who, no matter how complex the computer and printer or how detailed the instructions, manage to whip the equipment out of the box, connect all the cables, and start using the machine in a matter of minutes. But for the rest of us unfortunate mortals, setting up the computer can be a full day's worth of frustration, with at least three frantic calls to the service number for help and the onset of a glowering mood that discourages any suggestions from friends and relatives who happen to be in the vicinity. Observational research may not be able to find a way completely out of this technical morass, but it can help.

By observing and recording—moment by moment—the points of frustration, the inadequate digestion of dubious instructions, the mismatching of cable to port, the actions and words (even if unspeakable) that result from a printer's refusal to print, the whole process of dialing for help and being asked to stand by while other customers are being serviced, and having to explain the problem to one of those voices with an ever-so-subtle implication that you're just another non-tech moron, a company can go a long way toward correcting and making the out-of-the box experience user-friendly.

Mr. Gates and Microsoft notwithstanding, today's software programs are often even more formidable than the hardware, and the experience of installation and learning to use them can take hours and weeks of trial and error. There may come a time when we all connect directly to programs embedded and instantly available on the Internet, but until then, software will proliferate like bacteria in a nutriment solution. There is an ever-increasing opportunity for observational researchers to help make the software world a kinder, gentler place.

Observation in this case may be conducted over a period of weeks, with the observer present at program installation and then returning at intervals to record progress (or lack of it) as the respondent begins to use the new software. Objectives of the research needn't only be oriented toward picking up on and solving problems. The researcher can enlist the user to figure out ways the program can be made better, easier to install, faster to learn, with fewer steps and keystrokes.

Frustration seems built into the process of getting from one website page to another, exploring links, and finding exactly what you want. And that's good news for observational researchers. Watching people bumble from one icon to another and follow inadequate directions, revealing their feelings through facial expressions and grunts, and the obverse—watching them use an intelligently designed, easy-to-follow website—will offer clear insights into the ways your website can be improved.

The researcher sits with the respondent as he or she attempts to find and navigate the website under consideration. Every time the researcher notices a hesitation or an error, the respondent is probed. Why the pause? What went through the respondent's mind when he or she clicked on the wrong icon? Where did the respondent really want to go? When all is said and done, was the website worth the trouble? Would respondents return to it in the future? If not, why not? What would make it more accessible? There is nothing like direct observation of the experience to find reality-based answers to these questions.

Broader studies of computer usage have revealed that, for some families, the computer has replaced the family hearth. When it is not used for homework, E-commerce or business, friends or family members often gather around it for games, looking up family-related information such as potential vacation spots and surfing the net.

PEOPLE AT WORK

Observation should not be confined to the home computer user. Office networks—from the E-mail experience to the transfer of files to the control of security and more—can benefit from close study of flow and process as employees communicate with their coworkers and with distant offices.

Researchers working with systems engineers *before* a new network or hardware is installed can help organizations save months of frustration and expense. How are employees using the current system? What are the problem points? What needs to be changed? What parts should remain unchanged? Day-to-day observation of individual users throughout the organization will provide valuable background for the open-minded engineer assigned to upgrade the network.

Website design and its architecture have become more and more in demand as companies use the Internet to sell, to communicate with customers, and to communicate between departments. Here, too, close observation of the stumbling blocks can point the way to improvement.

The computer is not the only potential office target of observational research. Imagine a hidden camera facing the copier. Is the machine providing angst-free output or is the office staff frustrated with its creaky service? What would it take to make the copier more useful for the organization? Watch a time-coded videotape of just one day's work, and you will probably learn the answers to these questions.

Other centers of activity such as the cafeteria, the mail delivery process, the phone system, and the everyday traffic that flows from one office to another are worthy of observation and study in the interests of efficiency and organizational morale. It is also useful for an outsider to observe and characterize what is commonly referred to as the *culture* of the company. It's hard for those inside the organization to step back and look at the company objectively, just as it's difficult for people to appraise and express their own salient characteristics. A trained observational researcher familiar with the various components and values of an office culture can help a company understand itself and present itself to the outside world.

TRAVELERS

For most people, being away from home—whether for business or pleasure—is a mixture of adventure and inconvenience. The observational researcher is ideally suited to understand and document the mix. In the eyes of the traveler, what parts of the experience enhance the trip? What diminishes it? The responsible factor could be something as small as a hotel food tray uncollected until the next morning, a squalid airplane bathroom after a six-hour trip to Europe, the special helpfulness of the concierge who knew exactly where to direct the guest who wanted a safe, quiet outdoors area for a few moments of meditation in the midst of a busy city, or the availability of a changing surface for babies in the airport bathroom.

Travelers may forget some of the specific details a couple of weeks after their trip. But it's the details that leave a good or bad taste in the mouth and that strongly influence a traveler's choice next time. The observational researcher can be of great help in uncovering the problem areas and the promotable positives and in capturing the details before they are forgotten.

How does a researcher observe and document the hotel, resort, or air travel experience? Not with a video or still camera. In the case of travel, it is best to leave all equipment, with the possible exception of a hidden audiotape recorder, at home. Here the job of the researcher is basically to travel as respondents travel, to hang out with them and observe them. Direct observation and conversation will tell you exactly what you need to know concerning what your fellow travelers liked and what they didn't like—in exquisite detail.

Want to learn what they think about a business flight? The researcher should dress like someone making a business trip, keep his or her eyes open, and start a conversation with a seatmate or with someone across the aisle. Often, a bit of praise or a complaint about the service will open the floodgates of reaction to what's happening or not happening and how the seatmate feels about it.

The same is true for a hotel or resort. The researcher will hang out in the café or restaurant or start up a conversation on the beach about the facility. He or she might begin with a dumb question like, "Do you know where I can buy a newspaper here?" and then watch the conversation turn to the service or the room or the food. After all, what else is there to talk about with other travelers?

Lest such an assignment seem like a boondoggle for the eager observational researcher, it should be said instantly that the real work is getting the comments down on paper or input on the laptop soon after the conversations and then organizing and making sense of the remarks and actions to help develop useful conclusions. This work is much more difficult without the aid of a videotape or an audiotape recorder. But this is one of the things a good ethnographer is trained to do.

An observational researcher can pinpoint the little touches along with the broad strokes that make travelers want to recommend a facility or an airline to their friends and to come back again themselves. The material will be abundant and highly useful in the development of advertising strategies and executions.

PEOPLE ON THE MOVE

American families move an average of at least five times in their lives. No matter how many times they've done it, a move is always traumatic. Understanding how people go about planning and executing a move at both ends can be very useful to moving, real-estate, and utility companies. What aspects do people feel more comfortable handling themselves? What seems to discombobulate them? Are the services offered to people on the move truly useful? Do companies take over a prolonged or labor-intensive job that families might have done themselves? Are services cost-effective? Are there still unexamined ways the companies involved can help make a move easier?

What people recall about moving and what actually happens during a move may be somewhat different. Here's a case where spending in-depth time with a family on the move—from looking for a new home to settling and closing on one, through packing up and heading out, through the trip to wherever, to unpacking, to contacting new utilities, and to inquiring where to go for essentials like food in the new neighborhood—can pay off. Such an effort will reveal problems and opportunities formerly taken for granted. It will also suggest potentially exciting new services for companies servicing this burgeoning market.

People and Social Occasions

Many products such as beverages, snacks, some foods, coffee makers, paper plates and cups, some music CDs or tapes, cameras, and certain fashions enjoy their greatest use and resonance in a social context. Parties, small gatherings at people's homes, large affairs such as weddings, corporate occasions, and even a night out at the local restaurant provide opportunities to watch a products effect on a number of people all at once.

The researcher will find many problems and benefits associated with a product at a social gathering. Is the paper plate a little too light for the casserole? Does the food threaten to slide off? Do people go for the macadamia nuts but not for the salted peanuts? Is the beverage consumption age related—diet colas and mineral water for the boomers and alcoholic beverages for the older people? If there's dancing, what kind of music is favored? Are there certain CDs people request more often? If someone's taking pictures, is the camera compact enough to be whipped out of a pocket when something interesting happens? Is there a certain style of dress favored at a party like this—a style a clothing maker or retailer would like to know about?

By assuming the manner and dress of others at the event, the researcher can pass as an invited guest and observe people using a product in a social ambiance. At many social events, it is even appropriate for the observational researcher to have a camera and openly take pictures, since such occasions often include at least one person recording the events for posterity. It is also appropriate to start a casual conversation about the product in question. "I don't know what Sue would have done without using paper cups, do you?" Or "I almost wore a dress tonight. Glad I came in slacks."

Social occasions also provide an opportunity to see how people relate to each other in particular age and income groups. What today's young people do at a gathering, the way they talk to each other, the way they dance, their body language, and the clothes they wear when they're together at the very least can give you the authentic background and setting you need if young people are expected to identify with your commercial. Whether your commercial is set in a bar or a playroom, the setting and the clothes had better be right—right down to the cuff (or lack of it) on a young man's khakis.

If you are talking, on the other hand, to people who are fifty-five to sixty-five (today's highest spenders in a number of categories), you will need to know a lot more about them than their retirement plans or their status as empty nesters. Many are poised for adventure—in travel, in restaurants, in cultural consumption, and even in the housing they select at this age. To know what's on their minds and to know where the next dollar they spend is going, you have but to spend a little time watching them live. Observational research will give you a feel for their lifestyle. And a social occasion is often a compressed statement of the way they live.

People and TV

There are a number of ways for broadcasters and advertisers to document consumer response to TV programs and commercials. But they are either quantitative or they bring consumers into an artificial environment such as a theater. As of this writing, no major research service provides the opportunity to watch and listen to every tiny but significant reaction to programs and commercials in a natural setting.

Would you like to know when consumers are rapt with attention to the screen or when they yawn, look away, get up, and go to the refrigerator or the bathroom? What makes them laugh out loud? What makes them nudge the people they're watching with to call their attention to the screen? And what makes them change the channel when they've had it with what they're watching?

Observational research can give you the answer to those questions. A videotape camera running on top of the family TV set, facing the audience, will show you a whole evening's worth of family reaction. What's more, you'll hear exactly what they're reacting to. And since the tape is coded for date and time—second by second, you'll be able to match up—instant by instant— a very specific part of the program or commercial to the videotape recording the respondent's reactions.

Minority Consumers

As anyone who has been involved with a major brand knows, marketing a product to minority consumers often requires a different approach than the marketing efforts used for mainstream consumers. Minority consumers not only often use products in different ways, but products also have different meanings in their lives. Recognized brands, for example, seem to be somewhat more important to African Americans than to many whites. And Hispanic Americans are more family-centered than are many white Americans.

But minority consumers don't fall so easily into broad categories like *African American* and *Hispanic*. Americans of Mexican origin have different values than those from Puerto Rico and, in turn, different values from those of Cuban immigrants. African Americans who have grown up in this country think differently from West Indians. Not to mention the generational differences among them.

There are significant differences between gay and nongay consumers in terms of product usage, purchase patterns, and attitudes toward products. And numbers of gay consumers without children enjoy a disposable income not available to others who are responsible for families.

It's a fact that many people in major corporations responsible for marketing to minority and gay consumers do not understand them the way they understand other consumers. And that's one of the gaps observational research can fill. A broad-based observational study can provide companies with a direct, reality-based understanding of each kind of consumer: how they live, how they shop, how products and services fit into the pattern of their lives.

Observational research can show precisely how the minority or gay consumer you're trying to reach uses and reacts to a specific product. The study will involve the same research techniques used on other consumers, but the findings will point out some important differences. In the experience of our company alone, we have seen usage differences in products as diverse as cooking oil, detergents, cameras, pet food, bathroom cleansers, cameras, and mouthwash.

Performing observational research on minority consumers raises an interesting question. Should a minority interviewer be used for minority interviews? If you are specifically seeking differences in lifestyle and usage, the answer is generally yes. Minority consumers sometimes tend to reveal more to someone who is considered *simpatico* because he or she is of a similar background. On the other hand, if you are including African Americans and Hispanic Americans, for example, in a larger study to obtain a representative sample of American life, a minority interviewer may be unnecessary.

GLOBAL OBSERVATIONAL RESEARCH

In observational research, the word *global* is probably a misnomer. As has been demonstrated many times over the past few decades, the same product positioning, advertising strategy, or execution and even the same product can be one country's meat and another country's poison. Though the global concept certainly works for technology and for some product categories such as soft drinks and some major brands of clothing, subtle differences in customs, mores, and social, political, and economic structures and values from one side of a border to another—and sometimes between one region of the same country and another—can affect marketing success or failure for most products.

For a corporation selling products on a global basis, it is vital to assess the local differences and to know the special attitude and usage idiosyncrasies of each market segment who will live with your products. Observational research is an ideal tool to help you learn such information in depth and detail.

As of this writing, observational research is being conducted by various research firms throughout Canada, England, and other parts of Europe and in parts of South and Central America as well as the United States. Recruiters, interviewers, and analysts are available with experience in the discipline. However, there are a few logistical problems to be aware of:

First, the quality of professionals can vary from very good to very bad outside the United States and Britain, and it would be wise to check them out before locking on a team. A safe bet would be to let an observational research company you have already used either manage and be responsible for your global projects or recommend a known firm.

Second, global observational research can present some language difficulties—particularly when it is conducted for a multinational company in various countries. Unless you are lucky enough to find a multilingual interviewer, you will probably have to use different interviewers for each country, taking the time to orient each of them to your objectives, interview guide, and methodology. The key responses will have to be translated into the mother tongue of the company funding the research when the findings are presented. When you are using audiotape or videotape, a secondary translation soundtrack running over the original responses solves the problem.

How Long with Each Respondent?

The length of time researchers spend with each consumer they observe can vary from fifteen minutes (in a store environment) to a week or two (for a lifestyle study). Some of the factors that determine the amount of time spent with each respondent are the scope of the inquiry, the number of respondents to be studied, the completion deadline, and the funding available.

Many packaged goods do not require cumulative observation. For in-home food and beverage consumption, paper products, cleaners, and some personal care products, one or two hours with each respondent or family are often ample. They provide time enough, for example, to observe and interview a person cooking dinner and then serving it to his or her family, complete with detailed evaluations from the family as well as the chef. And one hour is enough time to observe the effect of an antacid medication or the way a consumer uses a skin lotion. Spending a maximum of two hours at each home lets the researcher study twenty to forty respondents in various areas of the country, allowing for regional variations, and stay within a reasonable budget.

Other products take a while to produce their effect. The athlete's foot remedy mentioned in an earlier chapter required a return visit to sufferers when they had been healed. A study of camera users also required a return visit after the photos were developed so respondents could evaluate them. Products and services used in a variety of ways such as some computer-related products may call for multiple visits to the home or the office.

Sometimes understanding the lifestyle of a consumer is the key to developing the right marketing strategy. Trend- or fashion-related categories, everyday major equipment such as refrigerators or luxury cars, in-bar beverage consumption, and some personal electronic devices such as cell phones all benefit from staying with consumers for a period of time to develop an accurate assessment of the way the products fit or might fit into their lives.

Of course, living with a consumer all day, day after day, is both time-consuming and expensive. But the cost and time can be mitigated by pinpointing precisely the kind of consumer you want to study. Perhaps you know, for instance, that your primary customer base for a large, expensive refrigerator consists of suburban families with at least three children living at home and a household income of $100,000 per year or more, who prepare 70 percent of their meals at home. In such a case, fewer families might represent most of the manufacturer's customers. A video camera and a researcher watching the life of a refrigerator for two or three consecutive days in fifteen homes should give you insights valid for other similar consumers. (More discussion of lifestyle observation can be found later in this book.)

Another way of cutting costs is by sharing them. Extended studies involving lifestyle issues often have similar relevance for a number of product categories. In addition to the kitchen, venues that provide opportunities for multiple product study include the dining table, the bathroom, and the computer. Observational research firms can be helpful in bringing a number of clients together to find the same project—as long as the basic issues to be studied are the same or similar.

There are no templates in observational research. The way you go about your study should grow directly out of your objectives—what you want and expect to get from the research and how your findings are going to be used.

Housecalls, Inc.
200 E. 84th Street
New York, NY 10028
(212) 517-9039

Release Form

For valuable consideration (seventy-five dollars), receipt of which is hereby acknowledged, I and/or other members of my family agree to be present at an interview that will be videotaped as I/we change and discuss my hearing aid battery. It is understood that ideas, suggestions, or material may be furnished by me or others at such a gathering. These may be original or may be similar to ideas, suggestions, or material already in your possession which previously may have been considered by you. In any event, I give, grant, and transfer to you without additional consideration all rights to any ideas, suggestions, or material furnished by me for use by you as you see fit, without restrictions.

I understand that you may use the results of the interview or gathering for your own purposes, and I hereby release and discharge you from any claims, obligations, and liability of whatever kind of nature with respect to matters herein contained.

It is, however, agreed that my name and/or my family's name and likeness will never be broadcast on television or used in any advertising medium without my permission.

Name _____

Address _____

City _____ State _____ ZIP _____

Signed _____ Date _____

For Housecalls, Inc. _____ Date _____

(William L. Abrams, President)

THE RELEASE FORM

The researcher must have a release form signed by the respondent. It not only protects the research company and the client against potential lawsuits, but it also protects the respondent against unwarranted use of the interview. Here is a sample release from, which can be adapted to any kind of interview, including the in-store interviewer:

Your release should be on paper, and it should be kept forever. You never know when you may need to use a verbatim, a photo, or a section of video- or audiotape again. And you want to be protected. So, even if you have to put them in a separate storage facility, make sure release forms are easily accessible.

WHAT THIS CHAPTER TELLS YOU

- The way Americans bond with their cars is still relatively unexplored by the automobile industry. Observational research can turn up car-driver relationships that will push marketing beyond the classic forms so often used in automobile advertising.

- Anthropologists have descended upon the computer—both in the home and in the office—to explore in minute detail how a product or a process can be improved.

- On-site observation of air travelers and hotel patrons can reveal countless ways of improving service and encouraging repeat patronage.

- Minority consumers and other special groups often have needs and wants that differ from those of the mainstream— needs and wants that can only be understood through a detailed, close study of group members.

- Companies may not always be able to apply observational research globally. By its very nature, observational research is concerned with the particularities of particular people in a particular place. That's its value—and its limitation.

9

LOOKING FOR PATTERNS:

HOW THE FIELDWORK IS ANALYZED AND INTERPRETED

I n general, qualitative research differs from quantitative research in terms of the expectations placed on the project. With quantitative research, you look for definitive quantitative results: seventy percent of those surveyed felt the soap was too harsh. One out of three people preferred the mango flavor to the orange. Assuming your quantitative research has been set up appropriately, you can expect your findings to represent fairly and accurately what most people in the segment being studied will do or think—within a limited series of options.

It's unwise to place quantitative expectations on qualitative research and particularly on observational research—even though in recent years some reputable research publications have suggested there are instances when you can and should count responses in qualitative research. In most observational studies too few respondents are included to be reliably representative of a large market. More importantly, the primary reason you opt for direct observation is to understand the *quality* of the consumer's product experience. And the experience generally involves so many facets and layers that most of the time it's virtually impossible to quantify.

> Observation will provide insight and understanding that quantitative research and most qualitative research cannot duplicate.

A direct observation in-home study of beverage consumption was performed for a large company. You might think that determining the quality of the product experience in a case like this is easy—a person opens the bottle, pours a glass, drinks, and that's it. Not by a long shot. Here are just a few of the issues the research uncovered:

- Storage

- Relative position in the refrigerator

- How consumers buy it

- How they bring it home

- Who in the family drinks it

- Who doesn't drink it and why

- When they drink it

- How they drink it

  —from the bottle or the glass

  —fast or slow

  —diluted or straight

  —with or without food and what foods

- What they drink when they don't drink this product

- What benefits they see in the product

  —taste

  —thirst quenching

—energy boost

—health

- The image of the brand in their perceptions
- Whether they're drinking more or less than they used to and why
- What would encourage them to drink more

These are only some aspects of the experience probed in the study. If beverage consumption can include all these facets and layers, imagine the issues involved when observational research studies the preparation and consumption of a meal, taking a pet to the veterinarian, or setting up a new computer. The human experience—even when it concerns a simple product— is complex and multilayered. The more you understand it, the more your marketing efforts will speak to the consumers you want to reach and the more you will touch them on a deep personal level.

Let's assume the fieldwork portion of your direct observational research project has been completed. The recruitment has been successful and the interviews have been rich with opportunities for insight and analysis. The notes or photographs, audiotapes, or videotapes are ready for someone to plunge in and extract meaning and actionable conclusions. How is the material approached?

WHO SHOULD PERFORM THE ANALYSIS?

Should the person who performed the interviews be the same one who analyzes and interprets the material? Unless the interviews have been documented with notes virtually indecipherable to anyone except the researcher who was on the scene, it is usually better that the interviewer and the analyst be two different people. The interviewer is often so immersed in the interviews and so identified with the material, it is difficult to achieve perspective—even after a week or two. However, it's a very good idea for the interviewer and the analyst to exchange points of view as the fieldwork proceeds and after it's done.

The analyst should be thoroughly familiar with the objectives and background of the research and capable of discerning both the human nuances and product subtleties inherent in the details. But he or she also must have the strategic perspective to see the larger issues and ideas revealed in the interviews. Immersion in the day-to-day business of the brand can thus be a hindrance to understanding. Coming to the material cold, the analyst will bring objectivity and freshness of insight—a freshness hard to achieve by one who has been involved in the give and take of the interviews or the ups and downs of the product within the corporate structure.

Analysis in other kinds of market research is often given to junior people. This is not the case in observational research. The job should go to the most experienced person available—often the senior person on the project at the research firm.

To get the most out of the interviews, the analyst should relive them as he or she reviews them. The senses, the mind, and the associative capacities should be alert to every gesture, every word. The review should be equivalent of meeting respondents for the very first time. The analyst is ready to pick up cues from the way they dressed, the way they talked, the contents of their homes, and from their families, as well as what they did with the product.

An interesting psychological set develops while an analyst reviews the interviews—particularly if they've been recorded on videotape. When you're actually in the presence of other people, no matter how secure you may feel, you are conscious of the impression you're making. That consciousness goes away when you're looking at tapes. Because you can't make an impression on the people who are already interviewed and taped, you are free to be objectively interested in the respondents. Your judgments tend to be sharper and your reading of people more accurate. The ego disappears from your perceptions, and the result can lead directly to specific marketing ideas.

- In a study of single-use camera usage by eighteen- to twenty-four-year-old consumers, it was observed that many respondents spent a lot of their time in groups. Few interviews took place without at least one or two friends in the vicinity, whether in their homes, on the beach, at a roller skating rink, or in a store. The pattern prompted the research company and its client to see if the observation held true when it came to respondents' involvement with the cameras. It did. Three or four people often bought the camera together, took pictures with it, dropped it off at the drugstore for development, picked up the photos, and looked at them together. They even pooled their money to buy the camera in the first place. The concept of the group camera—owned and operated by a small number of friends—emerged clearly from the raw material, and was used in subsequent advertising.

FIGURE 9.1

The group camera concept emerged from observational research.

■ Quite the opposite took place when potato chip consumers were interviewed at lunchtime. Respondents were asked to eat lunch precisely the way they usually did—in the same surroundings and with the same people. After half the interviews had been completed, the analyst reviewing the material (videotapes in this case) realized that most of the respondents, whether they were in their homes or offices or in school, were enjoying lunch alone. The interviewer was asked to probe for the reason in later interviews. Why the solitary lunch?

It was found that many used lunch not as an opportunity to socialize, but to get away. They saw lunch as a time to collect themselves after a busy morning dealing with office demands, kids, or the classroom. It was a minivacation. And potato chips, with their aura of treat and indulgence, helped them escape and feel slightly irresponsible in the middle of a day filled with responsibility.

Most of the time, what people say in their own homes will match what they do. On their own turf people feel less need to prove something, less need to shore up their status when they respond to the interviewer's questions. But there are times when a dissonance occurs between words and action, and whoever reviews the tape must be alert to it. When they don't match, trust the action instead of the words. Ask yourself what prompted the consumer to say one thing and do another. For example, some hearing aid users, having a hard time inserting the tiny batteries while being watched by researchers, said they didn't usually have so much trouble. Listening to the tone of their apologies, the analyst concluded that they didn't want to be thought of as old and fumbling.

FINDING THE THREAD

Where do you look and what do you look for—the actions and words that differentiate one respondent from another or the common patterns? Eccentricities—the slips of the tongue, the bursts of unexpected emotion—are important. Look for the respondent who drinks from the bottle when everyone else drinks from a glass, the woman who puts a pump top from another product on top of a dishwasher detergent bottle, the computer buff who totally redesigns her desktop, the man who uses a deodorant all over his upper body, the kid who opts for a cereal that's less sweet.

Eccentricities can frequently give you dramatic insight into what's wrong with a product or how the product can be improved, or they can suggest a great new product idea that more conventional respondents only hint at. So, unlike the way you might discount anomalies in quantitative research, watch and listen for the oddball action or point of view. In observational research, such anomalies can produce golden results.

At the same time, the primary lines must be followed. Observational research may be the most qualitative of all forms of qualitative research, and it's meaningless to say that 73 percent of the observed respondents spent fewer than sixty seconds brushing their teeth. But noting that many respondents spent less than a minute with their toothbrushes is an important finding, particularly if you hear them say that their dentists told them to brush for at least two minutes. What's going on here? Do they think they're brushing longer than they actually are? Or do they trust their toothpaste and/or their brush to provide cleaning and adequate tooth and gum protection—even in that short time? Or do they think that other parts of their oral hygiene regimen, flossing and using mouthwash, for example, compensate for the shorter time spent with brush and toothpaste? In observational research, you have the opportunity to ask respondents why when you notice the phenomenon.

Keep your eyes and ears open as you go through the material, and the material will give the answer. Sometimes just watching what consumers do with a product—no words necessary—can provide the basis for a new marketing and advertising thrust. An observational study of a personal hand soap revealed people working the abundant lather into their hands as if it were a lotion. They continued to rub it in long after the soap had cleaned their hands. As the interviews were reviewed, it became obvious that the most salient attribute of the product was the lather. Respondents liked the feel of it, and they clearly thought it had a positive effect on their hands. This finding triggered a new lather-based advertising strategy. In due course, a new campaign was executed and it produced a significant rise in sales for the brand.

You want to be provoked. You want to be led to uses, ideas, positionings, and language you never knew were associated with your product. Although it may sometimes reinforce the status quo, provocation more often shakes you up. It makes you look at your product, your market, or your advertising as you may not have looked at it before.

Following a thread in observational research is an art perfected with experience, as already implied. Someone who has lived through a dozen marketing efforts—some successful, some unsuccessful—will usually have a well-developed nose for sniffing through the material. An experienced research, advertising, or marketing person will be able to extract an insight from a repeated gesture, see a potential problem in the place where a product is stored, or find an opening for a new product in a respondent's embarrassment over the rust on the bathtub drain.

It also helps if the one responsible for reviewing and summing up the material has the ability to connect seemingly disparate ideas. He or she may note, for example, that a respondent uses antibacterial liquid soap in the bathrooms and antibacterial dish-washing detergent in the kitchen and cleans the bathroom with an antibacterial cleaner. A consumer this concerned about germs might be a potential customer for a variety of new anti-bacterial products: an antibacterial underarm deodorant, an antibacterial floor cleaner, an antibacterial toy spray, antibacterial bandages, and even antibacterial sanitary pads to protect against infection, (assuming such products are medically sound).

A series of observational visits with families enjoying a dinner together revealed some of them remarking on children's conduct, politics, and the media from a traditional point of view. Invariably, these same traditionalists selected the oldest, most established brands of the packaged goods they used. This finding provided an insight useful for psychographic positioning and media placement.

I am sometimes asked, "How do you eliminate bias from your research?" The answer is, "You don't." You eliminate prejudice (literally, prejudgment). But in qualitative research of any kind, *bias* is another name for *experience*—the experience that tells you what to look for and where to find it. You want the bias of the analyst because, without it, all you have is raw information.

The raw material from the fieldwork should be made available to the client for whom the research was performed. The client may want to review the fieldwork and draw his or her own conclusions.

LOGGING MAKES IT EASIER

It may take time, but logging the responses into the computer as they are reviewed is an absolute necessity if fifteen or more consumers are studied (and your project shouldn't include any less). Logging consists of transcribing all the relevant body language, all the relevant verbal language, and all the relevant incidentals of the environment so that they can be used in your analysis and final report. In the long run, logging will save many frustrating hours and days of checking and rechecking the material. And it will make it much easier to find the patterns and to shape the presentation.

The fieldwork should be reviewed as it goes along—not after it's all completed. Reviewing as the material comes in from the field lets the analyst provide input to the interviewer for the interviews that follow. It offers the opportunity to add questions or follow a particularly interesting thread—a thread the researcher in the field may have missed.

Continuous reviewing is an objective control on the field-work, a control most often welcomed by the interviewer involved in the day-to-day detail of the project. If the interviews are logged from a video or audiotape recorder, the time code should be used to annotate words or actions as they are entered.

FIGURE 9.2

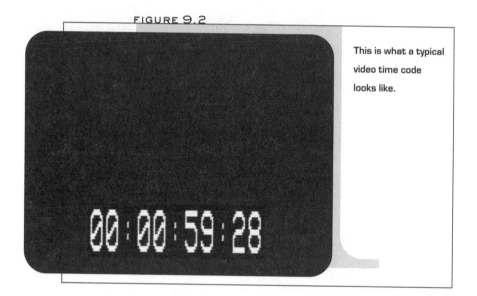

This is what a typical video time code looks like.

00:00:59:28

Obviously, some portions of the interview will be irrelevant or just connective tissue. But anything even vaguely related to the product, service, or issues involved should be entered. When working with videotape, you might enter words in upper- and lowercase, and actions in caps for easy reference when the analyst is ready to organize the material and write the presentation. The same words should be used to describe the same kinds of actions, so you can tell your computer to search for all similar entries later. You might use a special marking such as boldface for highly important words or actions.

When your words are on audiotape and your visual material consists of still photos, the analyst will connect the typed words to the appropriate actions. Small, reduced scans of the photos can be entered right alongside the words on computer. If all the analyst has are notes, they will have been categorized by the issues expected and revealed.

Making Connections

The primary job of the analyst is making connections—finding the insights and ideas inherent in the material. Here are two brief annotated portions of an interview from an observational research project on heartburn. The first portion was recorded on videotape after the respondent had eaten a tomato-based meal that gave her heartburn. The second portion was recorded by the same respondent on audiotape later in the evening, after the researchers had left.

Both segments were annotated by the project manager as he reviewed the material. The annotations are shown in the brackets.

Video (After Eating)

GESTURES.
My chest closes up from it. [Note her strong expression of symptom. Common to all?]

4:01:25
Felt it first in college, running quickly, eating the wrong foods. My life is stressful. Always in a rush. Like right now. WE HEAR A BANG AND A CRY. *You know that entire plate is laying on the floor, and the cleaning lady was here. Every night the big one will spill soda or milk, and the little one puts spaghetti on his head. Every night I'm choking on my dinner. If I could come in here and eat my dinner, it would never happen.* [Watch for relationship between stress and heartburn.]

4:05:28

*Went to dinner for my birthday at a restaurant called
Outback. They have the blooming onion. Said to
myself I'm gonna die if I eat this. But it's so delicious
that it was worth the suffering. 'Cause as soon as I
took the Zantac, I felt much better. But I knew. I went
there with the Zantac in my pocket and I knew I was
going to have to take it and I did. But it was worth it.*
[Note that she's willing to endure temporary suffering
for the sake of the food she wants, as long as
medication is with her.]

4:28:10

*This is the medicine cabinet in kitchen. Husband's
kidney medication. Son's prescription with Tylenol in
it. Lydex. Sudafed. Tylenol. Anbesol for my son's teeth.
My husband's Zantac 150 mgs. My husband's Swish
and Swallow. My Zantac.* (SAMPLES IN CUP) *Band-aids.*
[Family is medication oriented. Used to taking pills and
capsules.]

4:29:40

TAKES ZANTAC OUT OF FOIL (SAMPLES) POPS IT IN
MOUTH. TAKES WATER FROM FRIDGE, PUTS IN MOUTH,
SWALLOWS.

4:30:20

*I examine the floor and see my husband did a very nice
job of straightening up.* [Order, cleanliness important
to her.]

4:41:10

*Nobody gives me any time. No privacy. I can't go to
the bathroom in peace, have a headache in peace. Can't
be tired.* [She is on overload.]

4:44:15

I work myself up in a frenzy. [Stress oozing out of every
pore.]

4:45:00
I feel like it's (the pain) slowing me down. Don't like
that feeling. Like to get kids in bed by 8:00. Slows me
down mentally. Puts me in a bad mood. [She recognizes
effect of heartburn on her emotional life.]

Audio (Before Going to Bed)

It's 8:00, and I'm feeling somewhat more relief but not
total. (About 45 minutes.) As soon as I get the little boy
to bed, I'm sure I'll be feeling better.
[She connects absence of son with relief.]

It's 8:30. I'm feeling total relief at this point. My kids
are getting ready for bed, and it should be a very calm,
quiet evening here. Right now, I feel as good as I felt
before I started eating anything. Although it did take
the medication a little longer to work, at least it's
worked now. Hopefully, won't be any more discomfort
for the rest of the evening. [Seems that in addition to
medicine, removal of stress lessened heartburn
symptoms.]

It's 10:00 P.M. Getting ready for bed. I have no
symptoms of heartburn, feel great. [Clearly, symptoms
are tied in with demanding family.]
[Note: Which comes first, the stress or the heartburn?
Does one cause the other? How connected are they?
Possible larger promise available for the product—
reduction of the stress caused by heartburn. Unique
promise in the category? Watch for similar connections
with other respondents.]

Once the reviewer picks up the connection between stress
and heartburn, he or she will be alert for it in every subsequent
interview and return to those interviews already reviewed to see
if the connection was missed there. Stress was only one of the

threads followed in the heartburn study. This example shows how consumers experiencing the product and its benefits can open the door to ideas and connections not usually picked up in other forms of research. The notations indicate the kind of mental set the analyst might bring to the words and actions as they are studied.

ORGANIZATION—THE KEY TO UNDERSTANDING

Once the fieldwork has been completed and the interviews have been logged, the next step is organizing the responses—the actions and the words—under appropriate headings. The organization is the architecture of the study. The material will dictate the organization, and each study will produce its own unique organization.

Depending on the objectives, the organization might emphasize consumer reaction to the package. One heading may read "Hard to open," another "Extracts product easily," and still another "Storing problems," each accompanied by many illustrative, time-coded interview extracts.

Or your emphasis might be on lifestyle. For example, if you're studying beer drinkers at a local hangout, it might be interesting to note which brands are ordered by what kinds of patrons and why. You may learn that there are bonding beers and status beers and other beers that take the crowd through an afternoon of TV football. You might also discover that guys making a move on girls order a different kind of beer than when they're hanging out with other guys. An analyst would no doubt come up with dozens of other categories in the process of reviewing the fieldwork.

As the analyst works through the material and places the excerpts under various headings, he or she will notice a shape beginning to emerge. From the mass of interviews (some observational research projects have produced over one hundred and fifty pages of single-spaced, typed words), a series of insights will emerge, usually clustered around a general direction, heading toward the final report. The process is not unlike organizing and shaping material for a major paper in graduate school.

It's Not Exactly a Snap

It probably ought to be said at this point (as if it weren't obvious) that observational research takes work—a lot of work. Anyone planning to review the fieldwork and/or write the final report ought to enjoy this kind of scholarship—delving into detail and developing a point of view. Observational research requires close study to be valid and to be useful. A cursory review of the interviews is likely to produce cursory, inaccurate, misleading conclusions.

Are the detailed interviews and the time-consuming reviews worth it? You bet. So many unique marketing and advertising directions have come out of the insights derived from observational research, it is safe to say that this methodology has helped to change the fortunes of brands and companies throughout the world.

What This Chapter Tells You

- Observational research provides insight into the *quality* of the consumer experience—insight unavailable though quantitative research.

- Analysis of observational research fieldwork should be performed by an objective, disinterested senior analyst capable of strategic perspective.

- The analyst should bring an open mind to the material, looking and listening for the eccentricities as well as frequently repeated actions and words. He or she should be ready to connect seemingly disparate ideas.

- Logging the fieldwork as it is generated makes it easier to modify the approach, if necessary, while researchers are still in the field.

- The key to understanding is organization of the responses.

- You don't want the prejudice, but you do want the *bias* of the analyst. *Bias* is another name for *experience.*

10

PRESENTING THE FINDINGS:

MAKING THE INSIGHTS ACCESSIBLE

The way observational research findings are presented helps determine the degree to which they stay with their intended audience. In today's corporations, few decision makers have the time or the inclination to wade through a dense, fifty-page compilation of key words and summary points. Management wants it clear and concise.

But, please, it should not be too concise. An impatient audience with limited time (the usual state of affairs with top management) might want nothing more than a four- or five-page summary. And, in fact, a brief summary might be made available as a handout no matter what form the main presentation takes. But if that's all that is presented, the whole point of observational research will be missed: immersion in the close-up, personal relationship between the product and the consumer. The brief summary—if it's absolutely demanded—had best be a cut-down version of the full-length presentation, with the key points illustrated.

It's important to give almost as much attention to the presentation as to the analysis of the interviews. At one advertising agency, a researcher, who was a brilliant man with a strong academic background, was trying in his presentation to get across his analysis of the then-current detergent market. What he was saying was not only insightful, but also truly new—a difficult achievement in a category that had been looked at six ways from Sunday since the 1940s. The researcher was likely the first to identify the yuppie culture (no, he didn't invent the name) and to isolate the different needs and expectations young urban professionals brought to detergents.

The problem was the charts. He decided to "dramatize" his entire presentation with charts—thirty-six of them. Charts analyzed the current market and the current population. Charts isolated the urban professionals and their habits in other product categories. Charts projected that market into the future. All the ideas were worked out mathematically with graphs and intersecting lines.

Without question the man proved his point, and for its time the point was a breakthrough that could have helped to propel the detergent to a higher share of the market. But as his toneless voice droned on, explaining the charts and pointing out the highlights of his presentation, people actually nodded off. This breakthrough insight had the impact of a leaf falling into a mud hole. There was no response, no action taken. After a month, it was as if he hadn't ever spoken.

More recently, a presentation to an audience composed of market research and marketing people at a packaged goods company mostly confirmed what they already knew. But the presentation was so effective that it continues to be used as an educational tool for new people coming into the company and for certain outside suppliers.

> No matter what the style or who the audience, the better the presentation, the more the research will be used.

Types of Audiences

In general, observational research will be interesting to three different kinds of audiences—each with different orientations and needs. These are research and development, marketing and market research, and advertising.

R&D

Research and development people are a special kind of audience. While others may be interested in broad concepts or compelling visuals associated with a product, R&D wants facts—clear, uncluttered facts and specific detail. Precisely how long do respondents spend brushing their teeth? Do they brush their lower teeth longer than their upper teeth? Do they wet their brushes before or after the paste goes on? What kind of stroke do they use—up and down or from side to side?

The interviewer may often have asked, "Why?" R&D will be receptive to the answers, but they'll be more interested in the what than the why. Seeing exactly what happens when people use a product gives them the fodder they need to develop improvements or an entirely new product idea. Often, the second-by-second annotation or depiction of a specific action can show an R&D person precisely which direction the next stage in the product category might take. If you see people taking extra time to use peroxide in addition to a baking soda toothpaste, the next step is obvious—a baking soda toothpaste *with* peroxide. Watching one website user after another clicking on an icon that leads them to an unintended page or link should cause R&D to rethink the website design.

For R&D, the specific actions, habits, and practices of consumers that have been observed should dominate the presentation. The motivations, the broad marketing ideas, and the advertising execution potentials should take a backseat. The revelation that some consumers swish their mouthwash for thirty seconds may produce a yawn among advertising people, but it could be an exciting piece of news to a member of the R&D department.

Marketing

Marketing people—brand and category managers, market research people, and strategic planners—want a translation of the interviews into strategic concepts. Should the pasta be positioned as a side dish or a main course? What is the hierarchy of the purchase decision, what are the considerations that motivate consumers first, second, and third? Should a new use for the product be considered? What are the attributes consumers look for—size, flavor, or brand name? And what primary benefit should be communicated—taste, nourishment, fat content, or convenience? Are respondents willing to pay a premium for perceived superiority?

Observational research may not be able to provide definitive answers to these questions, but it can point the way. On the basis of strong responses from twenty-five or thirty consumers, observational research has the right and the obligation to suggest a strategic direction along with major consumer motivations, benefits, and other broad marketing-oriented ideas. These ideas and directions, documented with relevant examples from the fieldwork, should dominate the presentation. But no matter how clear the conclusions, and how right the strategy might seem, it is incumbent on the powers that be to check them out quickly and inexpensively.

Advertising

Advertising involves a variety of people: creatives, market researchers, marketing specialists, media experts, and management people, among others. They want everything that marketing wants and more: the benefits, the broad ideas, and the strategic direction. In addition, they look to observational research for execution clues—fodder they can use to help them create ads, commercials, and website communications that reach right into the kitchen, the bathroom, the computer room, or wherever products are used and considered. They're interested in the language consumers use when they talk about the product, the little gestures they make as they use it, the settings they use it in, and the countless items, rituals, and routines that make up the texture and context of the consumer-product relationship.

A presentation to advertising people should be idea-oriented, but the ideas should be ones that can be used readily in advertising—motivations, communications strategies, significant benefits discovered in the course of the research, new positionings that might make potential consumers look at the product in a whole new way. And the presentation should be a gold mine of verbal and body language respondents have been observed to use in connection with the product, language that could help the consumer identify with the product and other product users.

Knowing the orientation of the audience will help shape the presentation—whether you're the one who writes it or the manager who directs others what to write. What do you do when the audience includes all three—R&D, marketing, and advertising people? There is no choice. The presentation will have to be more comprehensive and probably longer. It may be necessary to break it into sections, so that each audience can decide to attend only the part of the presentation relevant to them.

PRESENTATION STYLES

The best kind of presentation is one that can be left with the people for whom it's intended so that they can use it whenever they wish and show it to whomever they wish. There are at least two presentation styles.

Still Pictures and Audiotape

Researchers of an academic or anthropological orientation often like to spend more time studying fewer people, preferring to explore the relationship between consumer and product in great depth and detail. Their tools, as outlined in the second chapter, are likely to be the still camera, the audiotape recorder, and the notebook. These tools dictate the style of presentation.

Anthropologists frequently use PowerPoint or large bulletin boards to arrange the many photos they have taken around each respondent in time sequence. First we see a photo of the pantry and its contents. Then we see a woman taking out the cooking oil from the second shelf. Here she is taking the lid off the oil. And here she is pouring oil into the saucepan. We see a snapshot of her cooking the sausages and then another of her putting them on individual plates. At the end or bottom of the board, we see the family eating the meal, including specific reaction shots as they bite into the sausages.

Near each picture are key quotes from the respondent relating to the action or issue depicted. These quotes may or may not be accompanied by snippets of audiotape at an appropriate point in the presentation.

The photos and the quotes are reinforcements of the key findings, point of view, ideas and suggestions, which are usually made by the researcher in an accompanying talk. Often, the anthropologically oriented researcher will leave behind an album or CD-ROM of copies of the photos and quotes along with a hard copy of the talk.

Videotape

Recording the interviews on videotape offers an opportunity to shape the presentation dramatically, pointing out key findings with multiple, representative interview excerpts. A videotape with edited excerpts can be developed to accompany the presenter's talk. A copy of the talk and the accompanying videotape are left behind.

A particularly accessible way to summarize findings is to create a documentary videotape, organized according to key issues, complete with narration and liberally illustrated with interview excerpts. This kind of summary contains everything that needs to be shown and said. It may run anywhere from thirty-five minutes to an hour and a half or more. Its advantage is that it can be copied and distributed to any interested party, without the presenter having to be there. And it can be shown again and again—either in its entirety or in part.

Here are a few brief portions of a script. The script was developed for a study of a product prototype—the same noodles and meat coating combination referred to in the screener in the recruitment chapter (brand name and company are once again disguised). It's included here to show you a workable format. From this script, an editor who has all the raw footage can put together the videotape summary unsupervised.

TITLE:

"An Exploration of Consumer Reactions to Brand Name Prototype"

TITLE:

"Videotaped among users of prepackaged, flavored dried noodles, pasta, and rice."

TITLE:

"For Company Name"

TITLE:

"See written summary for recruitment specifications."

TITLE:

"The People"
WOMAN IN KITCHEN, CUTTING CARROTS.

16:39:35
I do everything very fast. I'm actually in slow motion right now. I always feel like I'm in a hurry. I have to go to work. I have to do this. I have to do that.

Announcer: *Our respondents live in a world in which time is the most precious commodity. Those who work and those who don't both see themselves as busy and pressured.*
WOMAN COOKING.

19:29:37
That's the way my life is. I'm running, running, running. Who I've got to pick up . . .

HOLD SILENT.

Announcer: *They perceive themselves as having little or no time for cooking—with the possible exception of weekends.*
WOMAN NEAR PANTRY.

2A-3:34:17
If one thing is even five minutes delayed it throws everything off. It gets to the point where you time it. Getting home at six eighteen, and I'll have dinner on the table by seven thirteen . . .
WOMAN AT TABLE.

20:26:31
During the week I'm too busy to try anything new. That's why the cookbooks sit up there.

TITLE:

"The Product in Use"
WOMAN READING DIRECTIONS.

2A-303-17
Seems simple enough. Seems quick.
WOMAN COOKING.

19:16:58
Very convenient. Everything's right here. It tells you what to do, one, two three. It's requiring one pan for

the chicken and one pot for the sauce and noodles.
WOMAN COATING CHICKEN.

1:07:54
It's coating nicely, very easy. It's really going on better than bread crumbs.
XCU CHICKEN JUST OUT OF OVEN.

5:33:26
It looks like it should be cooked longer.
WOMAN EXAMINING COOKED CHICKEN.

18:33:60
Doesn't look like it's brown. I don't know if it's supposed to get real brown.
WOMAN STIRRING NOODLES.

6A-7:32:01
Smells good. Like it has Parmesan cheese in it.
WOMAN AND DAUGHTER TRYING FINISHED PRODUCT.

20:40:33
It's good, mama. Very good.

This material represents only a small portion of the script. It also contained a section in which consumer-perceived product benefits were visualized and verbalized, followed by suggestions for strategic positioning.

Whatever the style of presentation—audiotape, still photos, or videotape—the raw material should be made available to those who use the study. They might want to review specific interviews in more detail than a summary allows. An R&D client recently digitalized a project's raw videotapes and put them on CD-ROM, so that the material could be available instantly to research managers responsible for product development. The documentary summary too can be put on CD-ROM for the same purpose. In addition to the summary and the raw material, a few clients might require a hard copy on paper, "just for the record."

The Cost of
Observational Research

Now that the fieldwork has been done, the material organized, and the findings presented, it seems a good time to talk about the costs of observation research. On a per-respondent basis, this kind of research is more expensive than other forms of qualitative research such as focus groups. The in-depth nature of the interview demands that researchers spend a longer time with fewer respondents.

But looking at the cost of observational research on a quantitative, per-respondent basis is not the way to evaluate it. It should be evaluated on the unique insight, depth of detail, and direction it provides. Observational research is the only reality-based, in-depth research available for many key usage-oriented and lifestyle issues. It is the only research that probes the consumer-product relationship in intimate, personal detail. You will find that it pays for itself many times over in terms of the insight, veracity, information that can be turned into action, and mistake prevention it provides.

Depending upon the number of respondents, the incidence of product usage, the time spent with each respondent in the field, and the method of recording and presenting the material, the cost can run anywhere from $15,000 for a simple in-store project to $70,000 for a major on-site study of consumers across the United States. As of this writing, most studies range from $25,000 to $45,000, exclusive of travel costs in the field.

What This Chapter Tells You

- Presentation style is important. An uninteresting presentation can ensure that the findings fall on deaf ears. A good presentation involves the audience.

- R&D, marketing, and advertising people all have different needs from observational research. The presentation content should accommodate the audience.

- Presentation styles vary from still pictures and audiotape to video documentary.

- On average, the costs of observational research is about thirty-five thousand dollars.

11

NEXT STEPS:

WHAT TO DO WITH THE FINDINGS

After your observational research study has been completed and you've identified some previously undiscovered usage patterns, benefits, new product ideas, lifestyle issues, or strategic possibilities, what next? What do you do with the insights and information?

Some companies use observational research to set the direction for quantitative research—for large, definitive studies of a brand throughout the United States. In these cases, they might look to observational research to raise significant questions rather than to suggest answers. But most companies look to observational research to uncover potential answers to marketing problems or new marketing, advertising, or product ideas. And they want to find out quickly if these answers or ideas are projectable.

TESTING THE FINDINGS

If the research has generated a new or modified strategic direction, a positioning or repositioning of the product, one commonly used way of checking its validity is through concept testing. Concept statements are developed generally in multiples, with a few embodying the new strategy or positioning and one embodying the old or current strategy. The idea is to see if one of the new concepts beats the current concept.

Concept statements usually consist of a headline and body copy, enhanced if necessary by a simple visual. Here is an example of a concept statement, derived from an observational research study of cereal buyers and consumers, ready for testing.

Background: Research often observes parents and young children fighting over the cereal of choice at the breakfast table. Most young kids want something very sweet. Parents want something very nourishing. But finally there comes a time when kids are a little older and ready to accept something less sweet. The concept of this cereal capitalizes on the transition. It attempts to position the cereal against the point in time most will recognize. It needs no visual reinforcement to get the idea across.

INTRODUCING THE BREAKFAST CEREAL THAT TAKES THEM FROM VERY SWEET TO VERY GOOD FOR THEM

Finally, the day has arrived when you can get them off those multicolored, chocolate-coated candy-for-breakfast cereals and on to something a lot more substantial. They'll love this new corn and wheat cereal for the rich, sweet crunchy taste of grain, and they won't miss all that sugar one bit. And you'll love the ten essential vitamins and minerals they're getting with every spoonful. Finally, no more milk turning color and no more sugar at the bottom of the bowl. You'll be amazed your kids will love something so good for them.

There are a number of ways concept statements can be tested. One way is through one-on-one interviews set up through mall intercepts. Shoppers who represent potential customers are screened and brought into a facility just off the mall where they're asked for reactions to the concepts in return for a small fee or gift. This can be an effective means of finding out how numbers of consumers respond to the idea. However, in recent years we have seen more and more of the "wave-off" phenomenon. Up to 80 percent of those approached by researchers looking to recruit mall shoppers for a few minutes of questioning literally wave away researchers before they get a chance to say a word. The mall intercept has become an overused and therefore abused recruiting method.

Another way companies test concepts is through focus groups. Groups of eight to twelve consumers are brought in to look at concepts and discuss them. Reactions tend to be more detailed and richer than those from mall intercepts, but the dangers of peer pressure mitigate details. Is what respondents say honest, or are they saying it to make themselves look good to the other respondents?

If you test concepts in focus groups, beware of the bandwagon effect. Respondents will go along with the majority opinion so as not to seem negative or odd. Once, during the testing of an advertising concept in a series of three focus groups, a few respondents of the ten or twelve in each group reacted with great enthusiasm to the concept, and they carried the rest of the group. Yes, the idea was terrific. Yes, it made the product seem unique. Yes, they'd buy the product. Caveats and negatives were smothered under the overwhelming blanket of affirmations.

Even knowing full well that this reaction is not typical of people when they buy or use products, and recognizing the artificially induced hype, we too were caught up in the enthusiasm that came through the two-way mirror. There it was—*the* advertising concept we'd been looking for all those months. Didn't all those consumers agree?

Unfortunately, when the concept was accurately and engagingly translated into commercials and the advertising hit the media, consumers watching TV in their homes did not exactly react with the same enthusiasm as did those in the focus group. The campaign made a modest impression at best and, as for sales, forget about them. I would very much like to.

If you are going to test a concept through focus groups, be sure to bring along a large grain of salt. A better way to test con-

cepts might be on a one-on-one basis. Either prerecruit potential consumers and bring them into a facility and have them
react to your concepts individually or live with the wave-off
phenomenon and use mall intercepts to do the same thing. You
may have to settle for a briefer reaction from each consumer
than you'd get in focus groups, but it may very well be a more
honest one.

How many mall intercepts or prerecruited one-on-one interviews are necessary to determine that a particular concept is
viable? It depends on the comfort level of the company. Mall
intercepts are inexpensive. Prerecruited responses cost a little
more but still not much. A couple of hundred responses, with
two-thirds of them positive, should give you enough reason to
go to the next step. If the product has a regional skew, it's wise
to test in various areas of the United States.

Can and should concepts be tested via the Internet? For
Web-based products and Web-based retailers, this method is feasible—if you offer consumers, in return for participation, a
reward such as an item of merchandise, a credit, or check in the
mail. The advantage of testing concepts on the Internet is that
you are able to test directly with the specific individual consumers who are the most likely purchasers of the product in
question, assuming you have a customer list or an appropriate
database.

However, if the product or retailer in question is not Web-
based, you may be artificially skewing your responses toward
people who regularly use the Internet. In the case of everyday,
relatively low-priced products, the results from such testing may
not accurately represent your market. Another caveat: testing on
the Internet will not provide you with the spontaneous responses
available when the respondent is right there in front of you.

TESTING THE ADVERTISING

Ultimately, of course, even the most high-flown, breakthrough
strategic concepts uncovered through observation will come

down to the advertising. And the strategy will perform only as well as its communication. So it pays to develop a number of advertising commercials, print ads, Internet banners, or websites—different ways of executing the winning concept—and to test them to see which execution says it most convincingly.

When your observational research project has uncovered a hot new TV advertising execution—a piece of language or a unique visual that might capsulize what you want the product to stand for—what kind of testing is appropriate? Advertising executions should not be tested out of context. Develop a campaign and make a representative "down and dirty" commercial or a "stealomatic" (using bits and pieces from other commercials and print ads to get across your message). Use an advertising off-air testing service to get a relative score versus norms for commercials in the product category. This kind of test usually takes place in a facility at which people are exposed to commercials as part of a pilot television program. You'll learn what parts of your commercial interest people and what they remember or don't remember. The service will also give you the score on a persuasion index, which can be a good indication of the commercial's relative ability to push people into the store or to pull responses.

If your product is already on the shelves, you can test your new execution on cable with a limited, controlled audience. You're interested in two different campaign ideas? Use a split cable, in which half the TV audience sees one campaign and half sees the other. Later, they're queried to see what they remember and how it affected them and how the two executions compare. If you're advertising a product consumers write in for or order on-line, by putting a different code in the address shown in each commercial you'll get a clear idea of which one pulls best. You can have the same kind of testing performed on a print execution by means of a sample ad or ads created for a dummy magazine and for some actual newspapers and magazines. For advertising on the Internet, you can count the number of hits. Or if you're a retailer, you can add up the sales your website produced.

VERIFYING USAGE PATTERNS

Sometimes, all you want from observational research is insight into the ways people really use your product. The information is important for a number of reasons. The discovery of new uses can lead to significant new ways of differentiating products for consumers, new product benefits, product improvements, and even interesting new product ideas.

For example, consumers with cats were observed to mix a little baking soda in their kitty litter to absorb the odor. If baking soda did it for food odors, they figured, why not for stronger smells? The result, of course, was a packaged baking soda kitty litter.

And when a popular Internet provider was first introduced, the conventional wisdom within the company predicted that consumers would use the service primarily for information. However, observation revealed a very different story. What people who signed up wanted and what they used the service for was primarily social communication. This prompted the company to put a greater percentage of its technical and marketing resources into E-mail and chat rooms than into information sources.

Uses revealed through observational research can often be verified by means of a simple telephone survey. Do other people do what observed respondents were doing? Would they do it if they had thought of it? A survey can also be conducted in a store, among people shopping for an item within the product category. In certain instances, uses can be verified via the Internet.

Usage patterns uncovered through observation need not always make the earth move. Sometimes they serve simply as background material for advertising. When researchers found that pasta brought the family together, the information was picked up and used in the setting of the brand's TV spots. Families were shown in the kitchen, watching the mother cook and at the table enjoying—in these days of separate schedules and separate mealtimes—a great pasta meal together. It was an emotional hook.

What to Do with a New Product Idea

What do you do when observational research has turned up a new product idea and your company has some heart for it? You might ask your R&D department to make a prototype and then

FIGURE 11.1

Pasta can lead to family togetherness.

expose it to a couple of hundred people either by placing it with them in their homes or by bringing them into a facility and asking them to evaluate the product. As anyone knows who has ever had anything to do with new product development, this process can be expensive.

A number of companies these days—particularly those whose products are design-oriented—are turning to computer imaging. They develop clear, even three-dimensional graphics of new product ideas and present as many versions as is practical to individual consumers. Cars, home furnishings and furniture, various appliances, greeting cards, clothing, dolls, and some packaging ideas are all susceptible to computer testing.

An interesting aspect of the computer testing process is its potential for short-circuiting the new product concept test. Once you have a new product idea in one of the categories just mentioned, you can expose consumers directly to the product idea without going through the "What if there were a product that . . . ?" stage.

But if you have a new product that needs to be tasted, felt, worked with, or used as a remedy, you don't have the computer image option. To save significant R&D expenditures, it might be wise to develop, when possible, concept statements that explain the idea and test those first. For example, what if there were an inhaler—like an asthma reliever—you could use to relieve your headache in a matter of minutes? Or suppose you could use a skin lotion that not only softened your skin but protected you from skin-damaging ultraviolet rays? Or how about a digital thermometer you just place against your skin, and it gives you an accurate body temperature in just twenty seconds? These aren't necessarily serious or even original ideas, but they are the kinds of ideas amenable to new product concept testing for a fast, inexpensive reading of their viability. It's even possible to make a first test of a food or beverage this way—assuming the product has a strong concept value, such as a high-energy candy bar called *Michael Jordan*.

IDENTIFYING NEW MARKETS THROUGH LIFESTYLE

Lifestyle, or the way people live, has become increasingly important in today's marketing and advertising. In the absence of meaningful product differences, many companies have chosen to go the route of identifying a particular lifestyle and associating it as closely as possible with their products or services. The thinking is that consumers will identify with the lifestyle and hence with the product.

It's hard for a product to "own a lifestyle," but observational research can be of great help in this regard. It can burrow into the texture of consumers' lives. It can show you how they spend their time and money. It can reveal the values that motivate them. It can tell you the kinds of appeals and benefits likely to induce purchase of your product.

To identify or develop a clear picture of a specific lifestyle, the researcher should virtually live with a number of consumers for a few days. Taking notes and/or taking pictures, observers should be right there as much as possible when the family grabs breakfast, when they run their errands, when they sit at their desks in their offices, when they play with their friends after school, when they get together for the evening meal, and when they relax in front of the TV or wherever in the evening.

What are their concerns? What are their values? To what does the family give most of its attention? Researchers will watch for body language, observe what people are wearing, see what they buy on a shopping trip, record the dinner-table conversation, listen for the casual remarks thrown out during the commercial break in their favorite sitcom. From the specific details, the kind of people they are and their values will emerge.

The more specific the details, the more possible it will be for the product in question to "own the lifestyle" when it is advertised. It was the specific lifestyle situations depicted in all those Folger's commercials that allowed the coffee to assert believably, "The best part of wakin' up is Folger's in your cup," and to "own breakfast" for the product. Watch almost any beer commercial. The setting, the kinds of people who are drinking the beer and how they're drinking it, the conversation that takes place all have specific resonance for the people who consume the product. The more real and the more specific the commercial, generally the more consumer identification that is possible.

From lifestyle studies, it is also possible to identify a previously unaddressed niche market segment that exists outside of the usual demographic or, for that matter, outside psychographic categories. In 1998, the Guggenheim Museum in New York opened an exhibit of classic motorcycles, treating them as iconic art objects but also informing visitors of their mechanical specifications in the accompanying placards and catalog. One of the interesting aspects of the exhibition was its audience. Members of Hell's Angels, their huge Harleys parked in front of the museum, mingled with Wall Streeters who owned British cycles and with professorial art historians. They'd often be found together in an unlikely cluster around an especially unique motorcycle, listening to a knowledgeable visitor give an impromptu rundown on its history and specifications.

One seldom has the opportunity to see such diverse types, all interested in the same thing, drawn together in one place. But observational research can bring them together in pictures and sound and, out of a welter of incomes, ages, and regional idiosyncrasies, identify a marketable cluster of consumers.

When a phone company investigated the various ways its consumers used its phones, the observations uncovered a diverse, emergency-vulnerable market—people for whom the presence of a phone was vital because of what could or might happen. The market included older people fearful of injury or sickness, drivers who could not afford to be without their cars or vans, children who spent hours of unsupervised time after school before their parents came home from work, and handicapped people of all ages. If an emergency of any kind occurred, their first thought would be to get to a phone.

But wouldn't it be safer and easier if they carried a cell phone with them instead of having to depend on one being available where they happened to be? Yes, said potential consumers, a cell phone would be handy for emergencies, but it might be too tempting to use it and spend a small fortune just to make ordinary calls.

That's when the company invented the emergency phone, a cell phone with just two numbers you could speed dial by pressing a button. One number was 911, which would get you the police, the fire department, or an ambulance, and the other was any number of your choosing (of a close relative, for instance). You paid a low price for the phone itself and then only for the service when you actually used it to call one of your emergency numbers. This strong new product idea developed directly from diverse lifestyle observation.

AFTER IN-STORE OBSERVATION—A STEP TOWARD QUANTITATIVE RESEARCH

What do you do with the data you collect from in-store observation? If you've watched and interviewed a sufficient number of consumers, and you've covered the different kinds of retail outlets where your product is sold as well as your regional bases, it is *possible* to treat your observational data *somewhat* more like quantitative research.

A few years ago, a beverage company that sold most of its product in supermarkets initiated an in-store observation research project involving one hundred and seventy supermarket consumers in two areas of the country. Each consumer was observed with hidden cameras while shopping the shelves and then interviewed briefly in front of an open camera about the motivations for selecting the beverages he or she was about to buy. The research produced a broad hierarchy of values: the importance of the brand in relation to the flavor, price, and promotion, nutrition factors, and the influence of various family members over the purchase process.

However, because there were so many beverage categories under consideration, the research company argued that the number of respondents representing each category was relatively sparse. Some quantitative affirmation of the findings should be made. In other cases, particularly when just one product in just one kind of retail outlet in a shelf environment that varies only modestly from store to store is under consideration, a hundred

consumers or more may be enough to draw some broad conclusions about the way people shop.

One thing needs to be remembered about in-store research.
It will tell you why consumers are buying the product that day.
It will not tell you how consumers are actually using the brand
on an ongoing basis. It will not tell you how it fits into their lives
and whether they're likely to buy it again.

The ideal structure of an observational study is sometimes
a combination of in-home and in-store research. You will learn
something from such a study about the entire consumer experience, from purchase right on through to the discarding of the
empty package.

RELATIONSHIP MARKETING

In many companies that sell consumer goods on an ongoing
basis (packaged-goods manufacturers, for example), relationship marketing has drawn a great deal of interest. There's too
much competition out there to invest marketing resources in
achieving just a single purchase. Companies want a continuous
and enduring relationship to their consumers, based on demonstrated understanding and concern for their specific needs and
preferences.

There are many ways to keep track of consumer preferences.
Today's technology can easily find out what people buy, how
often they buy it, and where they make their purchases. But
that's like having a relationship with a fellow commuter you see
waiting on the platform at the same time for the same train
every morning. You may know what he wears, what paper he
buys, and where he sits, but that's about all you know about
him. It is not exactly the basis for a long-term relationship.

To have an enduring relationship with consumers, you want
to understand how they *bond* with a brand. You need to plumb
their emotional and functional investment in your product in the
context of their everyday lives. Observational research can pro-

vide the depth of insight and detail that will enable companies to understand consumers in their personal relationship to a brand, to understand what a brand *means* to them. It can help companies hold the consumer's hand and not let it go no matter what the competitive pressures are.

You may remember a British program on Public Television that documented a number of English adolescents at regular intervals on through to manhood. It was called *7-Up*. Take a page from that program and identify twenty to thirty ideal consumers of a brand or product category, consumers who buy at regular intervals and who give evidence of brand loyalty, the kind most marketers would like to retain. Then conduct observational research at regular intervals in their homes to track their changes in perceptions, usage, and emotional attachment to your product as well as to competitive brands. You will have an ongoing understanding of your product's place in their lives and how to maintain that place throughout the vicissitudes and complexities of their changing lives and the changing marketplace.

BEING WHO YOU ARE

If you are the decision maker when it comes to using observational research, what you do with it ultimately depends on whether you're a left- or a right-brain person. If you often use your intuition to help you make decisions, you will tend to see the observational studies you do as authentic windows into the consumer experience. You will see them as a rich mine of insight and consumer-generated ideas. You'll tend to integrate observation with the quantitative analysis you've done and use it to bring the facts and figures to life.

If, on the other hand, you are someone who mainly looks for the logic in marketing and who trusts the numbers most of all, you may think of observational research primarily as providing usage data and fodder for others such as advertising creative people. An advantage of observational research is that it is adaptable to the needs and predilections of diverse marketing, research, and advertising people.

EDUCATING COMPANY PERSONNEL AND SUPPLIERS

In the process of performing observational research, researchers often explore just about every facet of the product experience. Even in the most narrowly conceived project—how consumers deal with the opening and closing of a particular package, for example—there will be a need to know who uses the product, where it's kept, and what happens to the contents. The by-product is frequently a broad-spectrum study of product usage, with insight into primary benefits and comparisons with competitive brands.

Whether the study was performed with still pictures or videotape, the presentation and supporting data are often used for educational purposes. Company managers and other personnel newly assigned to the brand can get a detailed, reality-based insight into the consumer-product relationship from the presentation. New advertising agency teams can achieve understanding and find creative fodder from the materials without having to sit through lengthy and sometimes misleading focus groups. The same is true for the company's sales promotion and package design suppliers.

And let us not forget the education of top management. They may know the company's brands in the abstract—how they fit into the company's broad marketing or financial picture. But particularly in a multibrand company, top management can find it difficult if not impossible to keep track of specific brand-based details. Observational research is a quick way to keep top management abreast of current consumer usage and reaction. And when planning time arrives, it can supply rationales for marketing and advertising decisions arrived at by middle management. The "why" of a suggested direction is right there—visualized so that someone unfamiliar with the nitty-gritty of a brand can see and understand instantly.

Understanding a brand or a product category needn't stop with the summary of an observational research project. There are those in the company who need to know every aspect of the consumer-product relationship.

CREATING A LIVING LIBRARY OF CONSUMER USAGE

A number of companies are using the findings of observational research to create observational research libraries of consumer habits and practices relating to their products—a library that can be accessed on any computer in the company's network. Whether the data is on videotape or on still pictures with an audio track, the raw material is digitalized and assembled on CD-ROM under the categories of interest to concerned parties. With a keystroke or two, interested company personnel are able to call up actual excerpts from the interviews—complete with sound and moving or still images.

If you were putting together a library for a company that makes and sells snacks, for example, you might want to arrange the data under the broad categories of who purchases and eats the snacks, when and where they're consumed, what they're consumed with, taste perceptions, health concerns, and broad end benefits such as fun, relaxation, and comfort. Each category might have its own subcategories as well. The findings would be updated from time to time as the competitive, economic, or social environments changed.

When someone in research and development wants to consider a new product, when anyone in marketing needs to revisit a strategy or make a reality check of an advertising execution, or when new people assume responsibility for the brand, the needed material is instantly available. If the observational research is updated every so often, the library can also be used to track changes in consumer product usage and perception over time. Has your brand of ice cream made its way to the front of the family freezer since last year? Are there half-used bottles of the detergent you make sitting on shelves in the households that buy a competitor's new brand? Are people flossing more thoroughly since that spate of news articles on the effects of gum disease? Are they living with more or fewer material expectations and concerns than they were two or three years ago? An up-to-date observational library can provide you with living, ongoing insight into these questions.

WHAT THIS CHAPTER TELLS YOU

- Insights, benefits, and ideas revealed through observational research can be verified inexpensively through concept testing in one-on-one interviews or focus groups.

- Advertising execution ideas discovered through observation should be tested in context—in a commercial or ad. Use off-air testing services for new products and split-cable testing or split-run testing for existing products.

- Usage patterns can be verified easily through telephone interviews.

- New product ideas turned up in an observational research study can be tested via computer imaging if the product is design-oriented.

- Observational research can identify new lifestyle markets.

- In-store observation can produce quantitative results.

- Observational research is a valuable tool for relationship marketing.

- Observational research can help educate a company's new personnel.

- A "living library" of observational interviews can be kept on CD-ROM so they are accessible to all company personnel.

12

OBSERVATIONAL RESEARCH AND THE TWENTY-FIRST CENTURY

Thirteen years ago, I stood in front of a roomful of graduate students and predicted the day was coming when their sons or daughters might be out jogging, a Walkman or its equivalent at their ear, and they'd hear a message that went something like, "Hi, Sue Fallerman! You must be pretty hot and ready for a little refreshment about now. Did you know there's a Coke machine coming up on the trail in just one-fifth of a mile? Just dial in your universal I.D. number and the Coke will be charged automatically to your bank account."

That day, or something very close to it, is already at hand in some of the media. Individually directed advertising is state of the art on the Web and in some print media. And it won't be long before TV and radio commercials will follow suit and focus on specific people instead of a mass audience.

The more specifically directed the communication, the more advertisers will need to know about the individuals who make up their market and not just about the consumer's demographics, or the number of times he or she bought a particular can of vegetables at a particular store. Ideally, if a company could study every waking moment (and maybe a few sleeping moments as well) of each potential purchaser of its products, it would know precisely how, when, and where each product might fit into and enhance each consumer's life. If such knowledge were available, imagine the possibility of pinpoint marketing, of advertising that never misses because it hits precisely the nerves known to be exposed.

Of course, that precise degree of knowledge about the consumer is impractical on many levels and may never be available. But observational research is getting companies closer to it every day. (We'll examine the "Big Brother" or privacy issue shortly.) First, let's review some of the technologies now in their incipient states that promise to bloom into full-blown opportunities in the twenty-first century.

SOME NEW TECHNOLOGIES

Video conferencing has already been applied to in-home interviews. Right now, for example, it is possible for a company in Illinois to watch a live in-home interview in Maine, using just an ordinary phone line to carry both the picture and the sound. While a videotape camera in Maine records the interview, a small box connected to the phone line sends the images and the voices as they are recorded to a video monitor at the Illinois company. Advertising and marketing people watching the monitor see and hear everything happening in the interview. In fact, using the same system, they can even communicate with the cameraperson or interviewer to amplify a question, to ask for a view of another part of the house, or to ask another family member to use the product.

This technology is still somewhat crude. The image tends to break up every time the camera moves. But the problem may already have already been solved when this book is published.

In the twentieth century, the Nielsen company trained hundreds of thousands of people to keep diaries of their day-to-day TV habits. What about keeping a living diary of your eating habits, without having to write anything down? Consumers who agree to participate will have slow-running video cameras focused on their tables for a week to document the food served, who eats what, and what gets eaten first.

Consider shaving habits. A camera at the bathroom mirror, activated whenever the respondent stands in front of it, records the sights and the sounds—to the last ouch—of scraping a razor across a face. Oral care stands to be explored in equal depth and detail.

For meals, personal care, driving, and other activities, technology in the not-too-distant future will be able to keep a continuous verbal and visual record. Observational researchers will be able to tell their clients how their products are used daily over an extended period of time.

Another observational research tool currently available, a tiny video camera, can be embedded in a respondent's hat or in his or her outerwear. Imagine using this technology to record shopping trips or a week's driving history. Unfortunately, there is no sound available with the camera as yet. But give the technology a year or two and see what develops.

In the twenty-first century, camera surveillance in stores of every kind may be used to watch how people react to the products offered for sale. The six-month in-store history of visual and verbal consumer reactions to a brand—the hesitations, the joys of discovery, the arguments between family members over what to select, the quick dismissal, and the total ignoring of a brand—can be documented. Companies and stores will be able to make more informed decisions about what brands to feature and how they might need to be modified for greater visibility. And the effectiveness or ineffectiveness of point-of-sale material can be monitored right at the shelf.

Technology already exists to follow and record the point-to-point journey of an Internet surfer on a remote computer (with the surfer's permission, of course). An observational researcher can watch as a respondent moves from one link to another and see whether surfing ends with action—such as ordering an item of merchandise.

Observational research, however it is practiced in the future, will get further inside the consumer's head than ever before. Researchers and companies will be able to put together closely observed consumer actions and detailed lifestyle with unfiltered, naturally expressed motivations. Industry will be able to understand more fully, not only how consumers live with products and services, but also why they do what they do with them. Those companies that already have adopted observational research have found that this kind of knowledge truly is a kind of power. They have developed a competitive advantage over rival firms, and this advantage is showing up in products springing directly from consumers' needs and wants.

The Privacy Issue

This is as good a place as any to touch on the privacy question. In the 1990s, although security cameras in banks and building entrances were ubiquitous and clearly cut down on crime and led to the apprehension of criminals, protests against other forms of public surveillance were raised from time to time. Cameras at busy intersections, for example, were considered by some people to be an invasion of privacy, even in neighborhoods with frequent accidents or drug trafficking. The privacy of communications channels such as the Internet and the multiple use of data-based names and addresses have become hot public issues. There has been talk of some privacy-protection legislation in Washington.

The issue, of course, has been hyped by the media. We never read about citizens who are grateful for the surveillance because it makes them feel safer. We only see and hear negative responses.

On a moral or ethical level, privacy in our society is regarded as an almost sacred issue. Phrases such as "the right to privacy" or "an invasion of privacy" or, even more generally, the notion of a "private citizen" is deeply embedded in the language of our culture.

However, our morals concerning privacy are one thing. Our mores are something else. George Bernard Shaw has remarked that, "An American has no sense of privacy. He does not know what it means." Indeed, we are the most studied, probed, and documented society that has ever existed on the face of the planet. We have an insatiable curiosity about each other. We devour magazine and newspaper articles about our fellow Americans. Witness the enduring popularity of *People Magazine*. And we soak up television programs about lifestyles—our own as well as those different from ours. And that's only the noncommercial half of our curiosity.

The research industry in America is truly phenomenal in size and number. There are over two thousand companies involved in market research in the United States, and these do not include freelance researchers or companies and advertising agencies with their own market research facilities. Large packaged-goods companies, for example, sometimes have scores of market researchers on staff. I recently spoke at a company employing nearly a hundred full-time researchers.

The fact is, our public utterances concerning privacy often diverge sharply from our practices. We expect to be studied, examined, probed, and recorded in our buying habits, our media choices, our occupations, and our leisure-time activities. And, for the most part, we accept it without protest and participate when we have the time, except in regards to two areas we consider sacrosanct—our financial and medical records—although we resent when any kind of personal information is extracted and divulged without our permission. We have a vague sense that all this information about us is going to lead to better products, better movies, more efficient communication—a better life for us all. And many of us will give fifteen minutes on the phone to answer the questions of a researcher we've never met, working for a company we've never heard of.

Recently, I had a chance to probe seniors concerning their willingness to provide their names and addresses on forms and questionnaires submitted to them by various companies. You might think that people in this age group would consider themselves more vulnerable and less willing to endure invasions of privacy. But, surprisingly, almost every senior interviewed confessed to supplying his or her name and address when asked. Their reasons? They felt that providing their names and addresses along with the information requested would in some way lead to better products, not only for themselves, but also for all consumers.

Moreover, even when observing affluent families, our company has never been discouraged from recording every detail of people's homes—including their cabinets and costly possessions—with a videotape camera. Nor have we encountered much suspicion when performing observational research in households with far smaller incomes. We have found respondents of most backgrounds to be willing to be studied in intimate detail.

Beyond achieving its commercial motivations, the research leads to a more materially fulfilled life for the majority of Americans—rich and poor. In addition to our society's needs for better education and better job opportunities, a better material life is another goal worth working for.

Observational research is no more intrusive than any other form of qualitative research that probes the habits, practices, and attitudes of consumers on a one-on-one basis. If you accept the idea that your credit card contains a history of your supermarket purchases, why would you have trouble accepting a camera watch you hesitate, reach for, and then pick up a product at the store shelf?

In-home observation never occurs without the expressed permission of the person or families being observed. The release our company's respondents sign is also signed by one of our officers who promises never to exploit the consumers' participation other than for research purposes.

We need to know what the consumer wants if we are going to make products less expensive and more accessible. If we did not probe into the lives and minds of the consumers we hope to sell to, we would spend far more time and money bringing products to market. And much of the extra cost would come out of the consumer's pocket.

In many respects, observational research is a more valuable aid to understanding individuals within a consumer segment than are other forms of qualitative research. It can and often does lead to better, more accessible products. And, because it is reality-based, observational research certainly offers the strong probability that companies using it will spend less time, effort, and funds pursuing false leads. At least some of the savings will be passed on to the consumer.

A Few Predictions

The New York Times (June 10, 1999) reported a prediction by Larry Prusak, executive director of the IBM Institute for Knowledge Management: "There's going to be a huge flourishing of industrial anthropologists in the next twenty years," he said, adding that this was especially true in the technology sector because companies were continuing to study technology's potential for mimicking human behavior. "We're in the infancy in this area, and I don't think anyone would tell you differently."

The flourishing of observational research will by no means be confined to the technology sector. Currently, a number of large packaged goods companies devoted to team management are sending team members—particularly those working on new ideas—along with an observational researcher into the homes and everyday environments of their consumers. They not only study the ways their consumers live with products, but also, when it's practical, try to participate in their consumers' lives, to get a firsthand feel for the consumer-product relationship.

Observational research will draw its practitioners from various disciplines—not just the academic community. One owner of a firm offering observational research is a former chef. Another used to be a store manager. But most freelance observational researchers and firms devoted to the practice will crop up from more traditional forms of market research, from marketing departments, and from the advertising business. People who have been on the line in commercial firms will bring a marketing savvy to their observations that their clients will find highly valuable. And, as more and more companies employ the technique, observational researchers will proliferate in major markets throughout the country. Growth will more or less follow the history of the focus group in America.

Some people in the marketing and research communities have suggested that observational research may one day replace certain forms of quantitative research—such as time-consuming and expensive attitude and usage studies. While quantitative research gives you the numbers, they say, observational research gives you the depth of understanding and connection to reality that is often representative of the market segment under consideration.

Ideally, this book has made clear certain caveats. While observational research does indeed give you the depth of understanding that is often representative of a segment, it should be verified by inexpensive quantitative research before the findings are acted upon in a marketing or advertising program, unless, of course, you are performing observational research in quantity, such as for a large in-store study.

Observational research may very well be on its way to replacing other forms of qualitative research, such as the focus group. An article dated August 18, 1997, in *Newsweek* made the point that, "Focus groups were avant-garde in the 1980s . . . but consumers have been so bombarded with ads that they unconsciously (or perhaps cynically) parrot back what they've heard in commercials instead of reacting to products spontaneously. Even more troublesome is . . . when one highly opinionated person drowns out the rest of the group." *Newsweek* goes on to say what advertising and marketing people are turning to instead: "Another favored method for ferreting out the true tastes of consumers comes straight from cultural anthropology, observing the natives in their natural settings."

And in December 1997, Dorothy Leonard and Jeffrey Rayport in the *Harvard Business Review* asked,

> *How can companies identify needs that customers themselves may not recognize? . . . A set of techniques we call empathetic design can help resolve those dilemmas. At its foundation is observation—watching consumers use products or services. But unlike in focus groups, usability laboratories, and other contexts of traditional market research, such observation is conducted in the customer's own environment—in the course of normal, everyday routines. In such a context, researchers can gain access to a host of information through other . . . research methods.*

For a few companies, observational research is still not a regularly used methodology—but only because they haven't tried it. Most companies who use it once use it again and again.

The future of qualitative research will more and more belong to observation. And the companies that use it will reap the learning and marketing rewards described in these chapters.

WHAT THIS CHAPTER TELLS YOU

- New technologies are already beginning to allow companies to watch consumers in real time—as they use and respond to products in their homes—right from the company's offices.

- Future technologies will allow researchers to keep a continuous long-running verbal and visual record of family meals, personal care, and other activities such as driving.

- The long-running in-store history of shoppers' reactions to a brand on the shelf will also be documented.

- Future observation will help companies get inside consumers' heads more than ever before.

- The issue of privacy is much discussed in our society. But Americans expect to be studied. Consumers of all incomes are willing to participate as subjects in observational research.

- We depend on knowledge of consumers to avoid costly mistakes and to give them what they want at a reasonable price.

- Universities and major business magazines predict a flourishing of observational research during the next twenty years.

- Observational research may not replace quantitative research, but it may replace certain forms of qualitative research such as the focus group.

13

FREQUENTLY ASKED QUESTIONS ABOUT OBSERVATIONAL RESEARCH

Here are some of the questions I've heard prospective clients ask about observational research over the course of more than fifteen years. I've always tried to answer them honestly; although enthusiasm for the discipline occasionally seeps through.

I've heard the methodology you're talking about called ethnography *as well as* observational research. *What's the difference?*

In strict academic terminology, *observational research* is actually a branch of ethnography. However, for the last few years the marketing community has used the two terms almost interchangeably.

Isn't observational research one of those "warm, fuzzy" approaches to consumer insight?

If by "warm, fuzzy" you mean the insights are vague, emotional, and hard to pin down, let me be quick to correct the impression. Good observational research supplies clear usage patterns, well-defined consumer attitudes and relationships to the product, and strong, consumer-generated ideas—ready for testing. Because it's grounded in the reality of actual consumer experience, observational research is probably the least misty of all qualitative research forms.

Our company has been using focus groups successfully for fifteen years. Why should I add or switch to observational research?

You need a successful experience with observational research to convince you. Try a side-by-side experiment. Compare what you learn from a focus group with a small-scale observational study of the same kinds of consumers using the same product. If observational research turns up better material, gradually introduce it for appropriate projects. You may end up using both methodologies.

On a cost-per-respondent basis, observational research is more expensive than other forms of qualitative research. What makes it worth the extra money?

Observational research is the only form of qualitative research that gives you the reality and depth of the consumer experience, the only one that shows you how consumers actually use, think about, and live with your product in their everyday environments. Considered just in terms of helping you prevent mistakes, observational research is one of the best research bargains available.

Is observational research one of those marketing fads that will fade away in the next few years?

While certain observational techniques are relatively new, observational research as a discipline has been around and used by the marketing community for over twenty-five years. And more and more companies—from technology to fashion to packaged goods—are making it part of their research arsenal.

Why do I have to spend money for an observational research company? Why can't I just send out a few of my own good people to some consumers' homes to see what they can see?

Apart from the likelihood that they lack the training to conduct and document an objective observational interview, have you considered how costly it would be to send competent professionals in your organization away from the office for a week or more?

You sound as if observational research and focus groups are mutually exclusive. Do I always have to choose one or the other?

Choosing one form of research by no means precludes the other. Focus groups can be very useful in generating ideas, opening up areas of inquiry, and, if you're careful, testing concepts and advertising executions. And there are times when it makes sense to use them instead of observational research. Some companies use observational research and focus groups hand-in-hand to shed light on different aspects of the same project.

I have a product people use differently in different parts of the country. Wouldn't observational research be impractical and prohibitively expensive for me?

The price is the same, and the logistics are simple. The only extra cost is travel for the researchers. Observational research has often studied consumers using one product in three or four different regions of the United States.

We make an OTC medicine for a problem that comes and goes. No one knows when. How can we document the actual consumer experience of the problem and the relief our product offers?

Give the consumers in your study an audiotape recorder and have them describe the onset of the problem when it occurs, the way they feel when the problem is at its worst, and then the relief they experience after taking your product. Then, when the researcher has listened to and analyzed the descriptions, you'll have a real-life understanding of the way your consumer suffers and the relief your product brings.

Our company's products are all high tech. If we use observational research, shouldn't the research firm be knowledgeable about our product category?

The observational researchers you use should be familiar with your category but not necessarily knowledgeable about it. One of the advantages of using an outside company is the understanding its people bring from studying other kinds of products. A research firm too immersed in your category may not bring the perspective that enables researchers to see problems and opportunities in an objective light, and parallel to others they've previously encountered.

My company needs to do a broad, comprehensive lifestyle study of consumers in our target market. Is observational research the right tool?

Observational research will give you a direct, reality-based, hands-on feel for your consumers—the way they live, the way they think, and the place of your product or product category in their lives. Nothing does it better. But, for a truly comprehensive lifestyle study, you will need to spend more time with consumers than you would for a simple product study. Be prepared for somewhat higher costs.

When our company needs research, we need it now. We want the answers within two weeks. Can observational research move that fast?

Most of the time, when it comes to in-home research, no. Observational researchers interview respondents at the times they actually use the product—not at the marketer's or research company's convenience. It is seldom possible to complete more than four or five full interviews per day. And, because of their depth and detail, they require more time to analyze than the results of a focus group. If push comes to shove, a small study (fifteen people) can be completed in three weeks.

In-store research is a different story. Three days spent in a supermarket or mass merchandiser will more than likely turn up scores of respondents (depending, of course, on the product category), and because the interviews are much briefer and in less depth, the analysis and summary can be completed in a couple of weeks.

I'm sold on observational research, but it's hard to sell it to my company. How can I convince my management to use it?

The best way is to ask an observational research firm that uses videotape to lend you a noncompetitive summary on tape that they completed for another client. It will show your management the kind of work they're likely to get, and it will bring observational research to life. Or, if such a videotape is difficult to obtain, ask any reputable firm that conducts observational research to make a presentation tailored to your management. If yours is a company that believes in research, it will be more than worth their while.

I want my people to get a direct, hands-on experience of the consumer—in their homes. How can observational research make that happen?

If your people have the time, you should opt for the team approach to observational research. A few people from your organization can accompany the researcher at each interview and help him or her assess the completed interviews at the end of each day.

Would it be possible to observe and interview just four or five consumers as they use my product in their homes?

Forget this idea. Recruitment could include two consumers who are total anomalies, representing nothing but themselves. To be reliable, the observational research sample should include at least fifteen respondents.

How can observational research make points for me in my company?

Use observational research to discover something about your company's consumer that no one else has discovered. Or use it to document an idea you're trying to sell. See what happens when you make your point with a living, breathing sample of a consumer in action. Watch management sit up and take notice.

APPENDIX

Following is a study of younger single-use camera consumers Housecalls, Inc. performed for Eastman-Kodak in 1997. Both the proposal and the complete videotape summary script are included.

Among the findings of this study is the discovery that younger people purchase and use single-use cameras in groups. Three or four consumers go to the store together, take pictures together, and go over them together when they are developed. These findings resulted in the Kodak "Pass along" commercial currently being aired as of this writing.

PROPOSAL

Objectives

- To provide insight into the place and benefits of single-use cameras (SUCS) in the lives of eighteen- to twenty-four-year-old consumers, and how they may differ from those of other SUC consumers.

- To help determine special needs—both met and unmet—in this age group.

- To help find out what special meaning and benefits are specifically associated with Kodak sucs for these consumers.

Methodology

Housecalls will videotape and interview eighteen- to twenty-four-year-old consumers while they use sucs in their everyday environments.

Detail

- Screeners and interviewer's guides will be developed for approval.

- **Recruitment** will take place in the San Francisco or Los Angeles area. Thirty eighteen- to twenty-four-year-olds who have used sucs at least twice before and who are planning to use them again shortly will be recruited: ten from nearby college dorms and fraternity houses, ten from attached-house complexes where young people often live, and ten from among those still living with their parents. There will be an equal mixture of male and female respondents. They may or may not own a permanent camera.

- Housecalls will accompany suc users where and when they use their cameras, and will videotape all aspects of usage—from purchase to film development. Usage occasions might include

  Peer parties

  Family gatherings

  Weddings

Showers

Sports activities

Sightseeing excursions

Outings

Photographing babies

Photographing pets

Classroom or work-related activities

Spontaneous, casual usage

- Twelve respondents will be **revisited** when their film has been developed. Camera will observe reactions to finished photos.

- **Probing** during the interview portions will include ongoing reasons for usage, satisfactions and dissatisfactions, purchase process, development, quality, and ultimate disposition of developed photos.

- Housecalls will **log** and **analyze** videotapes as they are completed, and will develop a script for approval before editing the videotape summary.

Delivered to Eastman-Kodak

- Summary on ¾″ videotape: Narrated and organized according to findings and with consumer-generated special positioning suggestions and consumer-generated areas for improvement.

- Written summary

- Raw footage of all interviews

Timing and Costs

From the day the project is initiated, Housecalls needs five to six weeks to complete this project, depending upon the incidence of SUC users and ease of recruitment.

Total fee: $XX,XXX +/− 10 percent, plus travel expenses for interviewer, cameraperson, and Housecalls management (if presentation in Rochester is required).

First half of the fee is due at initiation of project. Second half is due upon completion.

SCRIPT

13:14:35
OPEN ON LOTS OF GIRLS IN DORM ROOM. THEN XCU OF FEMALE RESPONDENT SNAPPING PICTURES.

13:15:20
RESPONDENT AND FRIENDS SNEAK INTO ROOM TO SHOOT GIRL SLEEPING IN BED.

(Laughter) I love it!

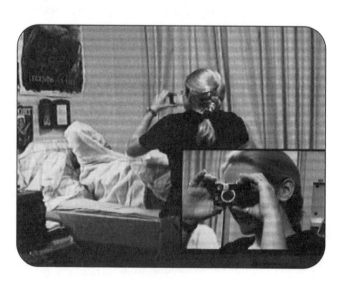

SUPER TITLE #1:

> *"Early Opportunities"*

> Announcer: *Early opportunities* . . .

CUT TO TITLE #2:

> *"A study of younger single-use camera consumers"*

> Announcer: . . . *a study of younger single-use camera users* . . .

TITLE #3:

> *(Housecalls Logo)*

> Announcer: . . . *by Housecalls Concept Development Systems for Eastman-Kodak.*

TITLE #4:

> *"Recruitment:*

> - *Thirty eighteen- to twenty-four-year-old male and female current users*
> - *Ten non-users"*

> Announcer: *Thirty eighteen- to twenty-four-year-old current users and ten who had never used an* SUC *before were recruited and videotaped in Orange County, California. See the written summary for recruitment details.*

TITLE #5:

> *"Issues:"*

Announcer: *This is a qualitative study, and therefore not projectable. But it does provide insight into a number of significant issues.*

TITLE #6:

"How do they buy?"

Announcer: *First, let's examine how our respondents buy SUCS. One answer—not always very easily.*

9:00:50
IN GROCERY STORE, MALE RESPONDENT GOES TO FILM SHELVES, LOOKS AROUND, TAKES A LOT OF TURNS, CAN'T FIND SUCS.

9:00:50
Respondent: *I know they're here somewhere.*

9:02:24
HE FINALLY FINDS THEM AT END AISLE. HE EXAMINES KODAK AND FUJI. HE PUTS DOWN KODAK, PICKS UP ANOTHER KODAK, AND COMPARES.

9:05:55
HE COMES TOWARD US ON A ROLLER BOARD WITH HIS CHOICE: KODAK.

9:07:25
I started browsing for this, 'cause it was kind of hard to find. Wasn't a section you'd assume there'd be. They were down low.

15:00:47
DISS TO FEMALE RESPONDENT AND FAMILY WALKING DOWN AISLE OF LARGE TARGET.

15:00:47
I think I have an idea where they are.

THEY COME TO A HUGE DISPLAY OF SUCS LOCKED
BEHIND GLASS DOORS.

15:01:34
SHE POINTS AT KODAK FLASH SUC.

15:01:34
The flash one. Want to ask the guy?

15:02:18
CLERK COMES TO UNLOCK CASE.

15:02:43
SHE PERUSES MOST UNITS, AND MAKES DECISION. HER
HUSBAND REACHES IN AND GETS CAMERA FOR HER.

15:02:43
I like twenty-four. The flash in the back.
CLERK LOCKS THE CASE AS THEY LEAVE.

DISS TO 4:13:38
A SURFER AT THE BEACH.

4:13:38
They didn't even know they had these. Guy was no help. No other brands of waterproof. No other brands of any kind.

4:13:30
I bought another waterproof kind—Kodak. Bought it at K-Mart. I went there first and they didn't have any more.

HOLD AND CONTINUE SILENTLY.

Respondent: *Contributing to the difficulty, as we saw in the previous study among older consumers, is a problem with graphic designation for some respondents . . .*

14:04:55
SURFER SHOWS POCKET THE FLASH.

14:04:55
Respondent: *They had a whole bunch of different kinds, and I wasn't sure of what to look for, so I figured I better get a flash. And something small and cheap. I lined up some—this is fifteen exposure. Don't need twenty-seven exposures. Were about three or four like this. All similar. Put them next to each other and picked. All kind of look the same. Have to look carefully to see what's best for each use. But on the rack, they all blend together. You have to spend time figuring out which is best for your needs. I was in a hurry. Maybe could have gotten a better one.*

12:10:00
SURFER COMPARES TWO KODAK PACKAGES.

12:10:00
(How are these different?) Oh, this one says "outdoor" only. And this one is outdoor, too. They're both by

*Kodak, so I don't know. Outdoor—daylight, oh, I
don't know what the difference is.*

HOLD AND CONTINUE.

Announcer: *A few respondents ended up buying the
wrong camera.*

11:26:00
Respondent: *I found out it was for outdoor use only, so
let's see if they come out.*

21:25:18
*I think I got the wrong kind. It would really be long
this way, or really long that way.*

HOLD AND CONTINUE.

Announcer: *Consumers who had problems during the
purchase process represent a significant minority of our
respondents.*

*For more respondents, the buying process went just
fine. There were many positive responses to Kodak
packaging and design—and particularly to that of the
new Pocket camera.*

104:09:45
Respondent: *Like how it shows exactly what it looks
like instead of having a picture on it. You know exactly
what you're getting.*
RESPONDENT COMPARING POCKET TO FUNSAVER
PACKAGING.

18:27:36
*This looks really compact. This one looks newer. Better
technology. The other is like a box. This one you get to
see the actual product. . . . I could also put it in my
pocket. Rounded. Plastic would be sturdier. I would
pay more because of the faster film speed.*

113:10:40
The way they advertise on the box. It has all the advantages. The gold jumped out.

Announcer: *A few even asked for and received helpful advice from the clerk.*

22:00:35
MALE RESPONDENT SHOWN IN DIALOGUE WITH CLERK
AT SAVON COUNTER.

22:00:35
Clerk: *Which kind are you looking for? Kodak or these kinds?*
Respondent: *Kodak would be good.*
LOOKS AT STORE BRAND.
What are the price ranges on these?
C: *Cheapest $5. On sale for 9.99, we got one with the new APS film in it. Have that developed here. Higher quality.*
R: *That one is better quality?*
C: *Yeah. Have your rewards card? Regularly 13.99.*
C: *Don't know if you know about APS. Instead of getting a whole bunch of negatives back, you actually get the roll back. And it tells you the negative numbers. And the prints comes out 4 × 7 for the same price as you pay for 3½ × 5. And this is a real nice one-time use camera. Actually has $2 savings. So comes out to 11.99.*
R: *I'll get that one, then.*

HOLD AND CONTINUE.

Announcer: *Cost is a big factor for many young respondents—bigger than it is with the older consumers we had studied—both at point of purchase, as you might expect, and as we'll see later on, when it comes to broader purchase decisions.*

11:02:22
FEMALE RESPONDENT PICKS UP STORE BRAND,
EXAMINES, THEN PICKS UP SAVON BRAND AND PAYS
FOR IT.

11:05:19
I picked pretty much by cost, which was cheapest. And this was on sale.

114:01:10
Know what you were looking for? Not necessarily. I looked at the price. Kodak was 16.99. This was half the price.

114:01:55
RESPONDENT SHOWS SAVON BRAND.

116:01:48
Looked at prices and compared exposures. Students have to save cost. Had most for the money. Twenty-seven.

116:01:48
RESPONDENT SHOWS STORE BRAND.

HOLD AND CONTINUE.

Announcer: *But despite the emphasis on cost, there is more reliance on brand name—and particularly the Kodak name—than we found among adults.*

0:10:01
Respondent: *Ones I've seen around is mostly Kodak. Good brand name, and you can rely on it. Comes out good.*

17:16:40
Kodak I always bought film from. Wouldn't want to go with an off brand. Might as well pay a little more money and get a brand I'm comfortable with.

107:01:00

*Looking for Kodak. Use it all the time. They had Fuji
and Savon brands, too. I've seen the most commercials
with Kodak. They're supposed to have the best pictures
and develop the best.*

HOLD AND CONTINUE.

Announcer: *Of the thirty current users of* SUCS *we
interviewed, twenty-one bought a Kodak brand to use
in this study. They were unprompted, and they did not
know the study was funded by Kodak.*

TITLE #7:

"How Do They Use SUCS?*"*

Announcer: *How do they use* SUCS? *For the older
respondents we studied previously,* SUC *usage was often
oriented to events or special occasions. For our
eighteen- to twenty-four-year-old respondents,* SUCS *are
much more a part of their everyday lives. And this is
especially true for our female respondents.*

13:12:36

FEMALE RESPONDENT SHOOTS PHOTO OF GUY AND GIRL
ON TOP OF BUNK BED.

7:36:00

TWO ARE SITTING ON ONE LAP IN BOWLING ALLEY. ONE
GUY TAKES SHOT. THERE IS LOTS OF LAUGHTER.

3:12:48

FEMALE CHEERLEADER WAITS WITH CAMERA FOR
BASKETBALL TEAM TO COME OUT.

3:15:30

SHE TAKES SHOT OF OTHER CHEERLEADERS IN
"ELEVATOR."

105:14:42
FEMALE RESPONDENT TAKES SHOT OF GIRLS ON SOCCER
FIELD.

105:15:35
GIRLS ARE PLAYING SOCCER.

116:16:10
GIRLS ARE PLAYING MINIATURE GOLF AND SHOOTING
PICTURES.

A9:05:22
MALE SKATEBOARDER SHOOTS FRIEND AS HE ATTEMPTS
TRICKY MANEUVER.

19:34:52
ONE FEMALE ROLLER BLADER HOLDS CAMERA OUT IN
FRONT TO TAKE PICTURE OF ALL THREE GIRLS.

19:05:05
*Everywhere we go we take a camera. I'm the picture
person.*

109:16:39
FEMALE TAKES SHOT OF GUY ON ROLLER RINK JUST AS
HE SLAMS INTO WALL.

118:27:40
FEMALE BABY-SITTER SHOOTS KIDS AMONG CACTUS IN
PARK.

15:26:34
YOUNG MOM KNEELS AT MCDONALD'S KID GYM TO
SHOOT HER CHILD.

15:14:50
I keep one in the diaper bag.

114:26:00
WOMAN AT A PARTY TELLS PEOPLE TO GET TOGETHER AS
SHE TAKES SHOT.

103:13:25
PICTURES ARE FRAMED ON DORM WALL.

103:13:25
*All over the wall at the beginning of the semester. Put
up the most recent.*

13:13:32
A DIFFERENT DORM WALL OF PICTURES IS SHOWN.

115:27:25
FEMALE WORKING IN DOG WASHER GETS DOG TO POSE.

115:23:25
*Taking pictures of people washing their dogs—for the
bulletin board.*

101:30:00
FEMALE TAKES SHOT OF CATS FIGHTING.

101:09:16
*I usually have a camera in the car. I always take
pictures.*

14:20:00
MALE TAKES SHOT OF PET IGUANA.

5:02:10
SURFER JUMPS INTO WATER WITH CAMERA AND SHOOTS.

5:02:10
SURFER IS IN THE WATER WITH BOARD AND CAMERA.

HOLD AND CONTINUE.

Announcer: *With few exceptions, female respondents
seem to take more pictures and like to keep them
around. SUCs and photos in general are part of
bonding. They are more important to their social lives.*

13:31:00
*(How important is taking pictures in your social life?)
Very. Anything that's any way meaningful, I take a
camera.*

101:41:50
*(Importance to social life of disposables on a scale of
1–5?) 4. I know I can always buy a disposable.
Pictures, camera very important to me.*

105:28:00
*I consider taking pictures easily without worry very
important.*

105:29:15
I pull out pictures once, twice a month.

112:34:15
*(How important are pictures to your social life?) 5.
With disposables? 5.*

HOLD AND CONTINUE.

Announcer: *For the men, on the other hand . . .*

1:09:00
(Basic use of disposables?) Activities, sports.

1:28:40
Respondent: *Like you could say once I jumped over a limo. That's proof. And proof in a picture is a lot easier than telling someone.*

18:07:06
A GREAT PICTURE OF RESPONDENT DOING BACK FLIP IS SHOWN.

18:16:40
I'll take my back flip picture and blow it up and make a poster of it.

5:18:50
Some days it's so good, and you'll have such good waves. You want to show people what you did. Some

*days it's so big. You can tell people about it, but when
you show people they're amazed.*

HOLD AND CONTINUE.

Announcer: *Both the young men and women we
interviewed associated* SUCs *with fun times and casual
usage.*

108:18:35
Respondent: *People aren't so serious with disposables.
Not thinking of serious stuff. More laid-back
atmosphere with disposables.*

19:38:10
*Whenever anybody's having fun, I think of a disposable
camera. So when I think of disposables, I think of fun.*

114:18:18
*You can use this more casually. Kind of snap pictures
off. The big one—*OK, *stand still.*

HOLD AND CONTINUE.

Announcer: *Sometimes the fun can get a little out of
hand. The respondents were unaware we were
videotaping this next sequence.*

20:25:00
TWO GUYS AND A GIRL USE THEIR KODAK FUNSAVER AS A
BALL, TOSSING IT TO EACH OTHER. IT HITS THE GROUND
HARD, AND THEY PICK IT UP AND TAKE A PICTURE.

20:25:10
Respondent: *Hey, it still works!*

20:26:00
THE CAMERA'S CARDBOARD TOP IS HALF OFF.

20:26:00
The packaging fell off. Never happened before. Still works. Pictures will come out. (Warning sound from camera.)

HOLD AND CONTINUE.

Announcer: *There's another phenomenon particular to these younger consumers, and it crosses gender lines. And that's the group camera.*

9:23:38
Respondent: *If we were taking a surfing trip, we'd probably all pitch in and share the cost.*

8:01:45
It's a group camera. Usually it goes around.

110:31:35
People are much more apt to share a disposable than a permanent camera. Very useful. People are much more into sharing. Not a lot of money.

HOLD AND CONTINUE.

Announcer: *Some respondents even buy, shoot, and retrieve finished prints together.*

19:01:18
THREE GIRLS ARE SHOPPING TOGETHER.

19:01:25
Respondent: *You got money? All I have is eight.*

19:02:45
We used this one when we went to Hawaii.

19:03:00
THEY BUY A FUJI.

19:04:38
We're good friends and we share everything.

19:05:00
*If we go out even to the grocery store, we, like, take
two or three people with us.*

19:06:54
Disposable? We'll pass it around totally.

19:07:00
*We split it. A lot of times we split pictures anyway,
passing them around.*

19:29:12
ONE GIRL ON SKATES TAKES CAMERA FROM FRIEND LIKE
A BATON.

HOLD AND CONTINUE.

Announcer: *Apart from friendship, money is the main
reason for sharing an* SUC *and the costs associated
with it.*

TITLE #8:

"Why do they use SUCs?"

Announcer: *Why do these younger respondents use SUCs?*

TITLE #9:

"Permanent camera owners:"

Announcer: *Those who own permanent cameras use them for some of the same reasons older consumers use them. For example, risk situations . . .*

14:41:15
Respondent: *I'll probably use this tonight. We're talking about going to Vegas, driving there. I'll bring this. Never taken pictures there. Be out drinking, having fun. Wouldn't want the permanent camera there.*

114:06:00
We have a very expensive camera, don't want to lose it. We go to the river a lot with our boat. Don't want to take the good camera on the boat. Don't want it to get wet, so we take these.

120:03:48
Friend's birthday. Decided to use a disposable because it's perfect. Won't use Mom's camera because we'll be out late. Don't want to break it or set it down and get stolen. Disposable is only ten dollars. Not worried.

HOLD AND CONTINUE.

Announcer: *And of course when they forget their permanent cameras . . .*

15:08:20
Respondent: *I have a permanent camera. It doesn't have a flash. We have a problem remembering the camera almost every time we go out of the house. . . . So we end up with a disposable.*

118:04:25
I have a permanent camera. I never think to bring it with me.

TITLE #10:

"Non-owners of Permanent Cameras"

Announcer: *Respondents also use SUCs because they don't own or can't afford a permanent camera.*

105:04:39
Respondent: *Don't own a camera. Have never been able to afford a camera. The disposable cameras are what I can afford.*

A9:22:00
They look like regular pictures. They're really fine. I'd take these to a formal. Not planning on getting a permanent camera 'til later. Just use these.

21:24:00
I've seen friends use disposables. Most don't have cameras.

TITLE #11:

"Acquisition of permanent camera reduces SUC usage."

Announcer: *There is fairly strong evidence—at least among our respondents—that when they do acquire a permanent camera, they use their SUCs less often.*

2:06:00
(Now that you have a permanent camera, will you still use portables?) Yes—if I ever use an underwater camera. Special occasions.

7:01:35
I don't usually buy them that often 'cause I have my own camera.

7:01:56
Say I'm going on a trip and I don't want to lug my camera around.

11:08:26
(Why do you use a permanent camera?) It was a gift. If I didn't have it I would use disposables.

13:04:38
I used to get them before I got a camera. Like if I went to running camp and I needed my own.

14:46:24
If these turn out nicely, I'll probably pick up another one. I'll still use a permanent camera in most situations 'cause I paid for the damned thing.

HOLD AND CONTINUE.

Announcer: *Most of these respondents have acquired their permanent cameras fairly recently. And it would be safe to speculate that they are still intrigued with its special advantages.*

TITLE #12:

"*But after they've owned a permanent camera for a while . . .*"

Announcer: *What happens after they've owned a permanent camera for a while? Sometimes the same thing that happened to our older permanent camera owners.*

19:23:00
Respondent: *I'm a newcomer to disposables. Coming out to college, I thought my regular camera was broken, so I bought a disposable. Then my mom sent me mine, and now I have two. A disposable is great just to pick up.*

22:07:50
(How long has your camera been broken?) Seven or eight months. I've used three disposables since then.

108:05:00
I have a permanent camera. Haven't used it in several years. Got it as a present. Don't use a camera much. Disposables four or five times a year. Camera I had was having problems. We got it fixed. Ever since, been leery about using it. It messed up shots on a trip. Rather have a fail safe camera.

TITLE #13:

"*Cost reduces* SUC *usage.*"

Announcer: *Another significant reason why our respondents don't use* SUCS *more often is cost. There's far more emphasis on this factor than among the adults.*

109:30:22
(What would it take for you to use SUCS *more?) If they were five bucks.*

107:13:55
If they were a little bit cheaper, I'd be more willing to buy SUCS *more often. They charge extra for the flash, too.*

106:12:08
Main thing with me is the cost, 'cause I'm a poor student.

21:15:30
Downside is price. A little more expensive. I have film at home in my own camera.

HOLD AND CONTINUE.

Announcer: *A number of our consumers figured out the economics of more frequent use . . .*

15:08:10
Respondent: *They're expensive if you do it often, but not once in a while. A role of film is half the price.*

13:04:25
You can buy a real camera for as cheap as $40, so if you spend $16 for each disposable, I don't think it's really worth it. I'd rather buy a real camera.

101:18:15
If you buy these all the time, you can invest that money in a camera.

HOLD AND CONTINUE.

Announcer: *There are some broad marketing implications suggested by these attitudes and practices, which we will express a little further on.*

TITLE #14:

"Projections: What kind of person uses SUCS?"

Announcer: *We asked our respondents what kind of person they think uses SUCS. Some of the answers were interesting, and they speak for themselves.*

106:16:45
Respondent: *Like my cousin. Too cheap to buy a permanent camera.*

114:43:30
When someone has a permanent camera and I have this, I sometimes feel awkward. "Hey—look at el cheapo over there."

9:39:38
Tourists use this kind of camera. You go to Disneyland, you see a lot.

109:29:50
Younger people on the go. Having a good time, not held down by a camera.

108:25:10
Parents have permanent cameras. Kids have disposables.

8:17:00
More kids than adults. Thirteen and high school.

118:15:30
Disposable users are last-minute people. That's how I wind up using it. Someone who's busy, like me.

TITLE #15:

"Satisfactions & Dissatisfactions"

Announcer: *What did they note that particularly applies—both positively and negatively—to Kodak* SUCS? *They especially liked the new Pocket camera design and functions.*

15:34:54
Respondent: *I like the Pocket because it's smaller and has a quicker flash. Hard to believe it's disposable.*

0:20:30
*Cool. This has an auto flash. Automatically recharges.
If you're taking quick pictures, it's already going.*

14:26:15
*(Best part?) Small and easy to use. Just hit the button
and it charges up every time.*

HOLD AND CONTINUE.

Announcer: *But not everyone likes the smallness of the
Pocket camera.*

6:17:10
Respondent: *It's smaller, so it's harder to make sure
your fingers aren't over the viewfinder.*

108:42:18
It's a little small for someone with bigger hands.

HOLD AND CONTINUE.

Announcer: *And eight respondents had trouble opening
the Pocket camera package.*

0:17:25
THIS RESPONDENT FIRST USES TEETH TO OPEN, THEN
USES SCISSORS, THEN SPENDS A LOT TIME PEELING OFF
PLASTIC.

2:07:45
RESPONDENT FIRST TRIES TO OPEN WITH FINGERS, THEN
HAS TO USE SCISSORS TWICE. HE THEN HAS TO RIP AND
CUT AGAIN.

2:18:24
Respondent: *The packaging was hard to open. I was
really struggling with it.*

HOLD AND CONTINUE.

Announcer: *As you saw earlier, they like the
availability of 800 speed.*

3:23:42
Respondent: *If we were roller blading outside, I'd probably go with this one because of the faster speed.*

HOLD AND CONTINUE.

Announcer: *But when a number of them looked through the viewfinder . . .*

17:07:30
Respondent: *When you're using a portable and looking through the little window, and you have the lines like on the nice camera, whatever you see in the box— maybe you'll get it and maybe you won't.*

101:14:15
Little eye view. Can't tell how far you're getting. On my camera you can adjust. This one you have to tell by steps. Harder to tell how far.

106:21:38
I notice a difference between the viewfinder and the final picture.

HOLD AND CONTINUE.

Announcer: *Perhaps it was California, or their age, but this was a very environmentally conscious group of respondents. Although most didn't notice the recycle symbol on the package, the idea appealed to almost everyone.*

9:36:15
Respondent: *I think recycle is like another one of those things. More attractive to have a recycled thing on there than not. Can't lose with recycling. Don't think this company does anything with recycling.*

11:37:05
I would rather choose a camera that's been recycled.
NOTICES RECYCLING SEAL.

118:45:20

I feel there are lots of parts to it that are, like, waste. I don't think they recycle . . . oh, wait. It does. I didn't know about recycling.

HOLD AND CONTINUE.

Announcer: *And with only a few exceptions, such as this respondent . . .*

1:11:00

Respondent: *It's always going to be a brand new camera every time you use it.*

HOLD AND CONTINUE.

Announcer: *. . . most liked the idea of reusing parts of an SUC.*

20:30:28

(If a company used part, would it change the way you feel about the company or product?) Sure. That I'd support. It wouldn't feel anything like a second-hand product. They wouldn't let something go out that didn't work.

105:29:40

I would be more comfortable with reuse. 'Cause then it's not wasting parts.

114:52:10

Reuse would be very good. I would consider that a motivation to buy.

HOLD AND CONTINUE.

Announcer: *By far the biggest complaint, and the most enthusiasm expressed to a suggested improvement had to do with shooting at a distance.*

3:19:30
Respondent: *I've noticed with disposable cameras, if you're too far away it doesn't come out. The ones that turn out best is if you're closer.*

107:10:15
A couple of times I took a picture and in the background it gets blurry. It doesn't come out too clear.

8:15:55
Zoom lens? Definitely would be interested. If you had two or three different settings, change it with a lever. I'd pay extra for it.

22:25:30
A zoom lens, that might be something nice, so you could vary shots. Might pay for it.

105:19:40
Get closer to the players. Would pay extra.

109:24:33
(Interested in a zoom lens?) Definitely. (Pay extra?) Would pay $1.50 for it.

HOLD AND CONTINUE.

Announcer: *A number of respondents also responded to the idea of an automatic advance.*

1:21:39
Respondent: *I like cameras that are automatic. You don't have to wind. Slows you down if you have to get action shots.*

5:11:00
If I could have, like, some weird one-button shutter advance, that would be great. 'Cause I have to hold my board.

9:27:08
(Would you be willing to pay for an automatic advance?) No . . . well, if it was really fast. Like a split second.

107:26:43
(Interested in an automatic film advance?) Nice. It's not too difficult to do it yourself. Especially if you wanted to take a couple of pictures at once, you have to stop after every picture to wind it, and then get something back in the lens. I don't expect too much of a portable. If they do come out with it, I would be willing to pay for it.

HOLD AND CONTINUE.

Announcer: *However, there were almost as many neutral responses as positive ones.*

8:13:45
Respondent: *Don't think an automatic advance really matters. . . . Not that much of a deal to turn the knob.*

19:42:18
It's not anything that's a big deal. Probably wouldn't pay more.

20:30:00
(Want an automatic film advance?) No, I don't want to pay $30 for a dumb little camera. You can buy a camera for $30.

HOLD AND CONTINUE.

Announcer: *Unlike the adults we interviewed, most respondents were reasonably satisfied with the current flash and the way it activated. Even those that weren't sure how to initiate it at first. A few were mildly interested in a lens cover that automatically activated the flash.*

112:17:45
(Would be interested in a automatic lens cover activating the flash?) I'd pay more.

8:15:30
It might be easier for a lot of kids and a lot of teens.

107:28:42
The flash is OK now. Works fine. Automatic wouldn't add much.

HOLD AND CONTINUE.

Announcer: *A few unprompted ideas for improvements came out of our interviews.*

1:26:40
Respondent: *The shutter should be a little higher. 'Cause you have to press your finger into it. It needs to be raised.*

15:14:00
(What would it take to get you to use it more often?) More pictures on a roll. For me—fifty.

11:23:10
The wind is really loud, so if you're in a quiet area, you have to put it behind you so it doesn't disturb anyone.

HOLD AND CONTINUE.

Announcer: *A number of respondents asked for an SUC that could shoot black and white film.*

106:17:25
Respondent: *I would use SUCs more if they had black and white.*

109:27:24
I'd be interested in a black and white disposable. I might use it instead of a permanent camera.

14:25:00
I think it would be nice if they had a little string attached to it so you could put it on your wrist and carry it.

SURFER DEMONSTRATES.

5:20:28
It's all right if you keep it around your neck when you're paddling, but when you surf it's too hard if you keep it here or on your arm. Maybe it could be strapped to your arm. Two straps and this would Velcro strap on. Or maybe on your wrist so you can takes pictures like this.

112:07:00
Don't think I've seen a waterproof with a flash. Pictures don't come out clear. Not enough light in the ocean.

112:07:40
One time I mixed one up. Don't know if they'd make like a different color. One time when we went snorkeling, my husband and I got ours mixed up with other people's on the boat.

120:24:10
What about a unit on the back you snap off and take in. You keep the plastic camera. So all you pay for is the film.

TITLE #16:

"Crossing the line"

Announcer: *There is an imaginary line beyond which an SUC has too many technical extras, and it costs too much. The line—at least for these younger respondents—has not yet been crossed.*

101:39:05
Respondent: *It would cross the line at $20 to $25. That might be expensive for people. But it would still be at a price range where they wouldn't have to consider buying a camera. I think the price is perfect now.*

106:26:05
(What is that line?) When they try to get too high tech with it. Automatic flash, wind, zoom lens would probably get expensive. Instead of buying it over and over again, I'd probably buy a permanent.

114:21:35
You could get a zoom and certain settings for lighting, but that defeats the purpose of being a disposable.

114:45:20
At the same price, they can add as much as they want. I wouldn't pay anything over $16.99.

115:42:32
It has not reached the line. . . . If you still had these, and then others with everything on it—a range, then OK. *But if you had a choice.*

HOLD AND CONTINUE.

Announcer: *The message from these respondents is clear. Improvements? Sure. But keep them simple and non-technical, and above all—affordable.*

TITLE #17:

"Perceptions of picture quality"

Announcer: *This age group tends to be both more suggestible and more discriminating about picture quality than the older respondents we studied.*

A few expected as good or better pictures than those shot by a permanent camera.

3:00:55
Respondent: *The pictures come out even clearer than when I had a regular camera.*

15:09:20
I don't notice the difference in quality between permanent and disposable pictures.

HOLD AND CONTINUE.

Announcer: *A few expected and got what they considered to be excellent pictures.*

22:32:05
Respondent: *I'm expecting high quality from this—the Advantix. Higher color and sharpness, the clerk said. I paid more for it than other Kodaks and I expect better quality.*

113:03:00
RESPONDENT OPENS ENVELOPE AND LOOKS AT ADVANTIX SHOTS WITH NEGATIVES.

113:03:00
I've never seen this before.

113:03:45
WE SEE PHOTOS—INCLUDING FOUR THAT DIDN'T COME OUT AT ALL.

113:03:45
I like the quality. Crisp—like right here. Really sharp. As good or better than permanent.

113:07:38
Next time I buy a disposable, I'll probably buy an Advantix. Looking at the pictures, the quality's good. Happy about what I got for what I paid.

HOLD AND CONTINUE.

Announcer: *What you see here is a man programmed to like the pictures—despite those that didn't come out—by the clerk who sold him the camera and by the extra money he paid for it.*

A few respondents got better results than they expected.

TWO FEMALE COLLEGE STUDENTS OPEN AN ENVELOPE. WE SEE THE PICTURES.

(Laughter) They turned out cute. Surprised they take as good pictures. That one's dark. Turned out a lot better than I thought.

HOLD AND CONTINUE.

Announcer: *But for many respondents, the underlying belief was . . .*

11:34:33
Respondent: *When you think of disposable, you think of less quality. 'Cause you're paying less.*

HOLD AND CONTINUE.

Announcer: *Resulting attitude . . .*

6:08:20
Respondent: *If I were just around my house I'd prefer a permanent camera, because I feel it takes better quality pictures. It's a more expensive camera. I haven't compared the two.*

112:09:50
Wouldn't expect it to be as high as permanent pictures, because the camera is cheaper.

18:01:38
What you pay for the camera, you expect the same quality. Not that great. Not as good as a professional

camera. Clarity of pictures wouldn't seem as good. The
plastic lens. Professional lens, crisp, clear colors.

HOLD AND CONTINUE.

Announcer: *One or two respondents founded their*
attitudes on a close comparison between SUC *photos*
and those taken with a permanent camera.

17:08:30
RESPONDENT COMPARES SUC TO PERMANENT PHOTOS.

17:08:30
Respondent: *Here's a close-up I did with that one, and*
here's a close-up of mine. See the difference? Much
clearer. I used a flash on both.

HOLD AND CONTINUE.

Announcer: *But most negative comparisons were based*
on the difference in cost between SUCs *and permanent*
cameras. Here's a man who believes in SUC *picture*
inferiority despite the evidence of his senses.

14:09:56

Respondent: *If I wanted real good pictures, I'd bring my camera.*

14:10:25

I'm sure there's a difference in quality. This can't take pictures like mine can.

14:13:48

My roommate bought one recently and we took pictures with it. That may have been a Kodak he bought. Pictures came out nice. Pretty comparable to pictures from a permanent camera.

HOLD AND CONTINUE.

Announcer: *Despite a predominant belief that SUC pictures are of lesser quality, they are good enough. Their standards, like their expectations, are lower when they use an SUC. And SUC pictures are quite acceptable for the money they cost and the uses our respondents put them to.*

106:20:35

Respondent: *I can do whatever I want and the pictures are going to turn out.*

115:12:12

When I don't need perfect pictures.

104:00:39

As long as they turn out—not dark or anything.

13:10:15

Anything is fine by me, as long as it has people in it and you can see them. I'm not real big on capturing the perfect sunset.

109:07:00
You don't get the highest quality pictures, but if you're just taking pictures of friends, they're great.

TITLE #18:

"*Non-users exposed to Kodak* SUCS"

Announcer: *We picked out ten younger people at random who had never used an* SUC *and asked them to try one. What we found was an immediate understanding of its ease and convenience.*

23:15:12
MALE AND HIS FRIEND ON THE BEACH WALK OVER TO A BOAT AND BEGIN SHOOTING.

23:15:46
Seems like a regular camera. Easy. Point and shoot. Automatic. No focusing. Seems cool.

23:32:24
FEMALE ON PIER READS THE DIRECTIONS, THEN WINDS AND TAKES PICTURE OF FRIENDS.

23:32:24
A Kodak moment!

23:33:25
That's fun.

23:33:45
It felt easy. Just push the button. Thought it was going to be hard. Thought it was going to be hard to use.

100:23:20
GIRL JUMPS INTO BOY'S ARMS AND GUY SHOOTS.

100:26:25
Easier than my camera. Manual focus in my camera. Have to set the flash, adjust the setting. This is snap and go.

HOLD AND CONTINUE.

Announcer: *They enjoyed getting their hands on the camera and using it for the first time. What quality did they expect from the pictures they snapped with the* SUC?

15:35:35
Respondent: *Pretty good. Because I've seen pictures from cameras like this and they come out good.*

23:12:00
Quality would be a disadvantage. Lesser quality from just looking at it.

100:02:50
(Why haven't you used it before?) A fear you're going to take something important and it's not going to come out because we've never used it before.

100:20:10
The pictures probably wouldn't be as good.

HOLD AND CONTINUE.

Announcer: *Despite the frequently encountered perception that* SUC *pictures would not be as good as pictures from a permanent camera, most new users expressed a willingness to buy one in the future.*

100:27:28
Respondents: *I'll probably buy a couple and keep them in the dorm.*

23:51:30
I would buy it in the future. I think it's pretty neat now that I've tried it.

HOLD AND CONTINUE.

Announcer: *What would they use it for? Primarily risk situations.*

23:37:24
Respondent: *I have my own camera.*

I do, too. I usually go to places where I'd need disposables. Where you wouldn't want to get your good camera hurt. Water skiing or something. The beach sometimes.

100:02:20
Good for day trips. Talked about bringing our camera or video camera, but we have a jeep convertible. Afraid someone might take it. Same with the video. This is something you can stick in your pocket.

23:19:30
For trips or something. To Mexico. If I go to the store and one's there. Sometimes I'm worried about breaking it (permanent).

TITLE #19:

"*Marketing implications*"

Announcer: *We have just a few key points to make in conclusion. First . . .*

TITLE #20:

"*Greatest* SUC *usage: Before they get their first permanent camera*"

Announcer: *Our respondents use* SUCS *most heavily before they get their first permanent camera. During this period, when they want to take pictures, it is virtually the only camera they do use.*

TITLE #21:

"They cut down on SUC *usage significantly once they acquire a permanent camera."*

Announcer: SUC *usage—at least among our respondents—is significantly reduced after they acquire a permanent camera.*

TITLE #22:

"Second greatest SUC *Usage: When Permanent Camera Disenchantment sets in."*

Announcer: *It may be a matter of years or a matter of months, but there comes a time when their new permanent camera isn't so new any more. It breaks, or they find it too bulky to carry, or they start to worry about risking it in problematic places, or they just forget to bring it. Then, like the adult respondents we studied, some go back to using* SUCS. *Although not as heavily as they had used them before they got a permanent camera.*

TITLE #23:

"Those who start using SUCS *early have the longest period of heavy usage."*

Announcer: *Those who start using* SUCS *early would seem to have the longest period of heavy usage.*

3:02:10
(How did you start using disposables?) Mom bought it for me because she says I lose everything. So, she thought it would be a good idea to get me one. Ever since then she buys them for me all the time, and I buy them.

106:00:39
My mom bought it.

115:12:50
First disposable my mom bought when I was thirteen.

120:06
Went to Florida. My mom bought me three before the trip.

HOLD AND CONTINUE.

Announcer: *A marketing effort to parents to convince them that their child's first camera should be a Kodak* SUC *might make sense.*

TITLE #24:

"Factors impeding greater usage:"

- *Cost*
- *Permanent camera acquisition*
- SUCs *seen for risk situations*

Announcer: *We've seen a number of factors impeding greater usage among our current eighteen- to twenty-four-year-old* SUC *users.*

Cost—both in terms of retail price, and when they start to use SUCs *frequently. There is a point beyond which it makes sense to buy a cheap permanent camera rather than continue using* SUCs.

And the acquisition of a permanent camera—no matter how disenchanted they may later become with it—also cuts down on usage.

Once they have positioned SUCs in their minds as cameras for risk situations—as many do, it also limits usage.

TITLE #25:

"It may be easier to get new users than to increase usage among eighteen- to twenty-four-year-olds."

Announcer: *There are new young people coming into the market all the time, and before they get their first permanent, they—and their parents—are most vulnerable to SUC purchase.*

We suggest, on the basis of this limited study, that it may be easier to get young new users than to increase usage among current young SUC users.

TITLE #26:

"Suggested improvements for young people"

Announcer: *Toward the goal of continuously interesting new young people in Kodak SUCs, and keeping them as heavy users as long as possible, we suggest first, that attention should be directed to the packaging.*

113:21:25
Designation on Kodak boxes not as clear as on Fuji. More to read. Boxes are similar, not distinctive.

TITLE #27:

"Clarify the packaging."

Announcer: *Kodak packaging should be clarified. Designations for outdoor and indoor, film speed, panoramic, and waterproof should be big, bold, and as visual as possible. Icons—a contemporary way of communicating, especially to young people—would help. But the distinctive Kodak yellow should always be part of the design.*

A problem noticed almost universally among our respondents . . .

19:08:50
Respondent: *Sometimes you're so far away and you want to get close, and instead of a button that makes the lens go closer, you have to like walk in.*

TITLE #28:

"Add a zoom lens."

Announcer: *More than any other improvement, they want a zoom lens.*

8:15:55
Respondent: *Zoom lens? Definitely would be interested. If you had two or three different settings, change it with a lever. I'd pay extra for it.*

HOLD AND CONTINUE.

Announcer: *Many expressions of a need for a zoom were unprompted.*

TITLE #29:

"Automatic film advance? Flash activated by the lens cap? Maybe."

Announcer: *We asked if they'd like an automatic film advance and a flash activated by the lens cap. The film advance idea received some strong interest.*

115:37:05
Respondent: *I'd pay a little more.*

HOLD AND CONTINUE.

Announcer: *It did not receive the same unprompted enthusiasm as the addition of a zoom.*

The idea of a flash activated by a lens cap received some assent, but little enthusiasm.

Some of the improvement ideas created by respondents made sense.

101:37:33
Respondent: *Black and white pictures. I love black and white.*

TITLE #30:

"Black and white exposures"

Announcer: *There seems to be a new interest in black and white film, and four of our respondents wanted the option.*

For those who take a lot of pictures, particularly on trips when it would be bulky to take many SUCs.

101:37:28
Respondent: *Maybe if they made one with more exposures. Maybe thirty-six.*

TITLE #31:

"More exposures"

Announcer: *We suggest the availability of more exposures in one* SUC *model—perhaps sold as a travel* SUC.

TITLE #32:

"Wrist strap for the waterproof"

Announcer: *And the surfer who made the suggestion of a Velcro wrist strap had a good idea. It's hard to swing an* SUC *off your shoulder and shoot while keeping you balance on the board.*

TITLE #33:

"Hold down the retail price."

Announcer: *No matter how many improvements are ultimately added, the top of the line Kodak* SUC *should cost at retail—at least for these young consumers—no more than half the price of the cheapest available permanent camera.*

A simple, no-frills model costing only a dollar or two more than a store brand, should always be one of the available options—perhaps with a special icon of a slashed dollar sign, or a symbol to that effect.

TITLE #34:

"A frequent user discount"

Announcer: *And in the light of respondent's concerns that frequent* SUC *use is uneconomic, why not offer a frequent user discount to this market?*

TITLE #35:

"Advertising to young people"

Announcer: *So often we noticed young people in these interviews spontaneously congregating in groups.*

9:17:50
SKATEBOARDER WHISTLES AT FRIENDS TO GET THEM MOVING, THEN TAKES PICTURE.

13:14:35
LOTS OF FEMALE STUDENTS IN DORM ROOM WITH SUC OWNER SNAPPING.

100:22:50
GUY BRINGS HIS SIX FRIENDS TOGETHER FOR A SHOT. A GIRL JUMPS INTO GUY'S ARMS.

HOLD AND CONTINUE.

Announcer: *And an SUC is often there—helping to make or support the fun.*

TITLE #36:

"Take a leaf from soft drink advertising."

Announcer: *We suggest that Kodak SUCs take a leaf from some of the great Coke and Pepsi commercials— where young people are having fun and bonding together—at sporting events, recreational sites, parties, and other gatherings. Occasions where the SUC has a chance to be present in numbers, and to add to the fun and the bonding—more authentically, in fact, than a soft drink.*
    Part of the campaign could depict the camera-sharing phenomenon we've seen in groups, along with sharing finished pictures.

It may be possible in the advertising to use real people in spontaneous group situations, as you have seen here.

Such a campaign might be entirely separate from advertising directed to adults—for example on MTV.

TITLE #37:

"Reinforce Kodak's SUC *finished picture quality."*

Announcer: *We've seen that one of the most widespread misconceptions among non-users is that* SUC *final picture quality would be inferior to that of permanent cameras. Advertising should reinforce the fact that Kodak's best film is used for its* SUCS, *and that final picture quality is excellent.*

TITLE #38:

"Accent recycling."

Announcer: *We also suggest, in any campaign directed to young people, that a pointed reference to Kodak's recycling policy be included.*

TITLE #39:

"Advertise to parents."

Announcer: *Increase the tendency of parents to buy* SUCS *as starter cameras for their kids.*

TITLE #40:

"Tie-in promotions"

Announcer: *We've seen our respondents often partic-*
ipate in various activities that suggest natural tie-ins . . .

TITLE #41:

- *Sporting goods*
- *Sneakers*
- *Sporting goods store chains*

Announcer: *. . . with manufacturers of sporting goods*
such as roller blades, skateboards, surf boards, wet
suits, bowling equipment, sneakers, and with large
retail sporting goods chains, for example. Offering
special, discounted SUCs *that display customized icons*
with sports equipment might be a good way to
introduce them to young people who haven't tried or
considered SUCs *before.*

TITLE #42:

"Completed February 1997 for Eastman-Kodak."

Announcer: *Completed February, 1997 for*
Eastman-Kodak . . .

TITLE #43:

"Housecalls Logo".

Announcer: *. . . by Housecalls Concept Development*
System.

Reprinted courtesy of Eastman-Kodak Company. KODAK is a trademark.

BIBLIOGRAPHY AND ADDITIONAL READINGS

Atkin, Charles K. "Observation of Parent-Child Interaction in Supermarket Decision-Making." *Journal of Marketing* (October 1978): 41–45.

Baldinger, Allan L. "An Observational Study of Children: Report on an ARF Pilot Project." *ARF Children's Research Workshop* (April 6, 1988).

Cochran, William G. *Planning and Analysis of Observational Studies*. New York: John Wiley & Sons, Inc., 1983.

Collier, Trevor. "Dynamic Reenactment." *Marketing Research*, vol. 5 (2): 35–37.

Gladwell, Malcolm. "The Science of Shopping." *The New Yorker* (November 4, 1996): 66–75.

Grove, Stephen J., and Raymond P. Fisk. "Observational Data Collection Methods for Services Marketing: An Overview." *Journal of the Academy of Marketing Science*, vol. 20, 217–224.

Helmreich, William B. "Louder Than Words: On-Site Observational Research." *Marketing News* (March 1, 1999): 16.

Krueckeberg, Harry F. "Customer Observation: Procedures, Results, and Implications." *Quirk's Marketing Research Review* (December 1989): 16–43.

Larson, Erik. "Attention Shoppers: Don't Look Now But You Are Being Tailed." *Smithsonian* (January 1993): 70–79.

Larson, Erik. *The Naked Consumer: How Our Private Lives Become Public Commodities.* New York: Penguin, 1994.

Larson, Erik. "Supermarket Spies." *Health* (September 1992): 59–66.

Leonard, Dorothy and Jeffrey F. Rayport. "Spark Innovation Through Empathic Design." *Harvard Business Review* (November–December, 1997).

Lewis, Peter H. "Forget Big Brother." *The New York Times* (March 19, 1998): G1+.

Mariampolski, Hy. "Solving the Problems of Observational Research." *Esomar Publication Series*, vol. 215 (July 1997): 51–65.

Mariampolski, Hy, and Claudia Schwartz. "Observational Research: Encountering Consumers in Their Natural Habitats." *ARF Qualitative Research Workshop* (June 18, 1996).

Rodgers, Alice. "Observational Research in a Focus Group Setting." *Quirk's Marketing Research Review* (December 1993): 28–29.

Rust, Langbourne. "Observations: Parents and Children Shopping Together." *Journal of Advertising Research* (July/August 1993): 65–70.

Suen, Hoi K., and Donald Ary. *Analyzing Quantitative Behavioral Observation Data*. New York: Lawrence Erlbaum Associates, 1989.

Underhill, Paco. "Kids in Stores." *American Demographics* (June 1994): 22–27.

Underhill, Paco. *Why We Buy: The Science of Shopping*. New York: Simon & Schuster, 1999.

Wagner, L. C. "The Use of the Observational Method in Marketing Research." *University of Washington Business Review*, vol. 27 (Autumn 1968): 18–24.

Welch, Lois Reiser. "The Purchase Decision Process and Naturalistic Observations." *ARF Children's Research Workshop* (April 6, 1988).

Wells, Melanie. "New Ways to Get into Our Heads." *USA Today* (March 2, 1999): B1–B2.

INDEX

ABOUT THE AUTHOR

Bill Abrams is the president and founder of Housecalls Concept Development System, the first qualitative research company to provide observational research on videotape to the marketing and advertising communities. Bill was the innovator of this system in 1983.

Housecalls has been featured in *Newsweek* and *The New York Times* and on the business segment of United Airlines in-flight videos.

Prior to founding Housecalls, Bill was a creative director for major advertising agencies, including Kenyon & Eckhardt, Ted Bates, and Bozell. He was a member of the board of directors at Ted Bates and Bozell.

He has taught advanced creative strategy at the University of Illinois and at Columbia Graduate School of Business. He is a member of the American Academy of Advertising as well as the Advertising Research Foundation and the American Marketing Association.